FIRST RUN
SHARK

FIRST RUN
SHARK

THE COMPLETE GUIDE
TO PORBEAGLE FISHING

Mike Thrussell

WARD LOCK

First published 1990 by Ward Lock
Villiers House
41–47 Strand
London WC2N 5JE

A Cassell imprint

Photographs by the Author, except pp 12 and 13 of
plates, courtesy of Russell Symons.
Artwork: Ian Foulis Associates

British Library Cataloguing in Publication Data
Thrussell, Mike
    First run shark: the complete guide to porbeagle fishing.
    1. Great Britain. Coastal waters. Sharks. Angling
    I. Title
    799.17310941

ISBN 0–7063–6930–0

Printed and bound in Great Britain by Butler & Tanner
Ltd

Contents

Introduction: First Run

Those of us who fish are fortunate – we are given a rare opportunity no other form of sport can provide. Fighting a large, powerful fish on a relatively weak rod and line creates a unique joining of two strong wills. On one side the fish, master of its own domain, using its powers of speed and manoeuvrability to break the angler's line; on the other the angler, reliant on skill, judgement of tackle, and patience of mind to subdue it. That thin connection of rod and line allows the angler to feel and to come to know the fish's strength and strategy; you feel its dives, head shakes, rolls, and twists, the sulks and sudden, dramatic change of speed and direction. The fish feels the angler pump the rod to regain line, tighten the drag forcing it to change course, yet always ready to take advantage when the angler allows the pressure to ease. Ultimately, one will feel the other weaken.

This is a marriage of two incompatible species – a union of opposing forces. No other sport (where human being and animal come together in opposition) has such permanence of contact yet freedom of will.

It is said that a person's real character is exposed when under pressure or open to an element of danger. Your own and your companions' souls are bared to all when sharks are the quarry. It's impossible to describe how it feels to fight a shark for several hours: you have to live it. Ninety per cent of anglers weaken within two hours, first mentally then physically. Yet the real test comes after three hours when everything hurts and only strength of will gets you through.

There is also fear. You worry because you don't want to appear weak in front of the others. More importantly, you don't want to let yourself down. This is a true adventure, and there are precious few left in modern times.

In learning about sharks I've made many mistakes, but learning the hard way is the best. Fighting a shark is a lonely experience: I hope some of my words stay with you and that consequently you don't feel quite so alone when your reel screams to that first run.

Mike Thrussell

CHAPTER 1

The Porbeagle Shark

Where the name 'porbeagle' comes from seems a matter of conjecture. The *Oxford English Dictionary* says its origins are unknown, its first appearance being in the old Cornish dialect. One possible origin could be the combination of two old French words meaning 'hog nose', which would tally with the *Oxford English Dictionary's* explanation for 'porpoise', referred to in Roman times as *'porcus piscis* (translated as 'hogfish'). The scientific name, *Lamna*, comes directly from a Greek word for a frightening man-eating monster; *nasus* (Atlantic porbeagle) means nose, and *ditropis* (Pacific porbeagle) means double keel, which refers to bodily characteristics described later.

Particular nicknames are associated with the porbeagle in certain defined areas. Bonito shark, salmon shark, and mackerel shark are local names derived from the prey upon which the sharks feed. Off the US coast of Maine, it is called the bluedog, whilst in Britain it is always called the porbeagle or porgie.

Porbeagles are at last being recognized worldwide by anglers as fine sporting fish. The sullen weight from their barrel-like bodies, coupled with bursts of speed spawned by their short, thick tails, provide an adversary both admired and respected. They are moody, taking bait slowly, often with a degree of gentleness that's hard to comprehend. Even when the angler sinks the hook they may not become alarmed but, at some stage in the battle, weight and speed come into play, the angler watching helpless as three, four or even five hundred yards of line melts from the reel spool. Sometimes unseen giants take it all.

The sudden burst of speed that catches sport-fishers by surprise is possible because the porbeagle is warm-blooded – its swimming muscles maintain a higher temperature than that of the surrounding seawater. Porbeagles are happy in temperatures as low as 4°C (40°F), yet the dark-red muscle tissue surrounding their spinal columns might read 12°C (55°F). The higher the water temperature, the higher the heat level in the muscle tissue. A threefold increase in power has been suggested for a rise in body temperature of 10°C. (Tuna, long noted for their agility and speed, are also warm blooded.)

The average length of the mature porbeagle is said to be 3m (10ft). Anglers' estimates of the size of fish are notoriously elastic, but having spoken to many reliable commercial fishermen, anglers, and divers (and from my own experience) I would increase this figure by 60cm (2ft). Porbeagles of 3.7m (12ft) are known but these are the exception – they exist and have undoubtedly been hooked. A famous skipper (who has seen many big sharks) brought to the side of his boat and subsequently lost a fish estimated at 3.4m (11ft) after a $4\frac{3}{4}$-hour battle on 36.3-kg (80-lb) class tackle. The estimated weight of the fish would be nearer 320 kg (700 lb) than 270 kg (600 lb). The biggest porbeagle I'm aware of that was taken on rod and line is Jorge Potier's 210-kg (465-lb) fish taken off Padstow, Cornwall, England, in 1976. Other fish approaching this weight have been taken in several other areas, mostly in British waters.

Other sharks can be mistaken for the porbeagle. In north-east American waters, the paths of the noted man-eater, the great white shark (*Carcharodon carcharias*), and the porbeagle cross. Blue shark (*Prionace glauca*) inhabit waters cruised by porbeagles in the summer months, as do makos (*Isurus oxyrinchus*).

Porbeagles are a dark grey or blue, shading to a pure-white belly. Occasionally, they are almost black across the back when they are caught in areas of rocky reefs. When taken over sandy banks, a mottled-brown effect may be noted around the fin and pectorals. Some specimens have a colour defect (about which, more later). The nose is pointed and overhangs the crescent-shaped mouth. The large, black eye is situated above and directly over the front of the jaw. There

are five large gill slits. Pay particular attention to the pectoral fin: this really only superficially resembles that of the mako. The mako's pectoral has a more slender shape and more length, coming to a slightly sharper point. This is even more exaggerated in the blue shark, which has a very long, thin pectoral.

The front edge of the dorsal fin is vertically in line with the rearward base of the pectoral fin. Viewed sideways, the dorsal curves slightly from the point before resuming a straighter line. Mako have a sharper tip to the dorsal, while the great white has an almost vertical rear edge falling from the dorsal's tip to the back.

The blue and porbeagle's dorsals are similar. However, the blue has a habit of showing both the dorsal and upper lobe of its tail when surface swimming, which the porbeagle rarely does. Basking shark also sit on the surface with the dorsal and upper tail lobe above the surface. When you see a large fin at sea, check for a very sharp point to the dorsal and look for that tail lobe – it may only just break water. A basking shark's tail lobe is slightly higher than the tip of the dorsal and can always

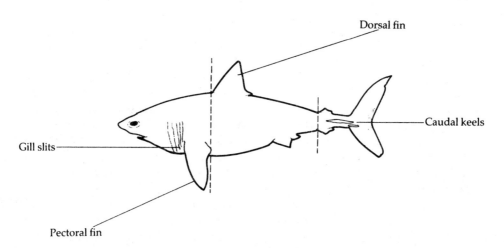

Figure 1a: The porbeagle shark

10

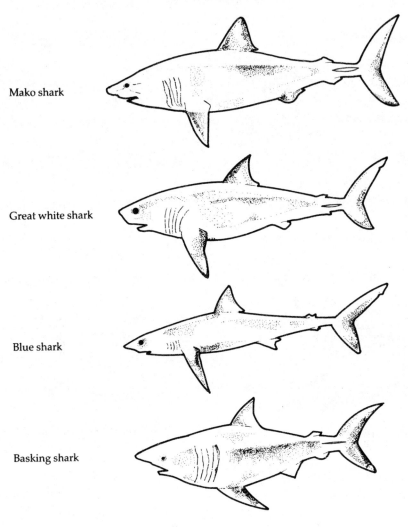

Mako shark

Great white shark

Blue shark

Basking shark

Figure 1b: Other species

be seen: a single fin with no other visible signs is almost certainly not a basking shark. The dorsal on a porbeagle also carries a telltale white spot at the rearward base of the fin. The general shape of the porbeagle is bulkier; the body weight is pushed forward towards the head and the tail has a slower taper, giving the shark a well-fed appearance in the water.

Once caught, identification is simple – the teeth are the give-away. These are single spikes with a small cusp at each side. None of the other sharks have these. The caudal keels are another clue. The upper, wide keel is found on other sharks but the smaller, secondary keel found on the lower lobe of the tail is unique to the porbeagle. These keels are also found on some of the mackerel family and the billfish, for which speed is an asset: sharks feed on mackerel, and they need to match the speed of their prey. The physical differences between the Atlantic porbeagle (*Lamna nasus*) and the Pacific por-

11

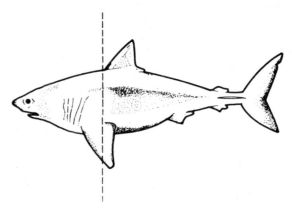

Figure 2: The Pacific porbeagle (Lamna ditropis); *wider pectoral fin*

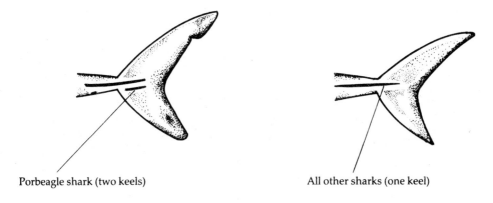

Porbeagle shark (two keels)   All other sharks (one keel)

Figure 3: Caudal keels of porbeagle and other sharks

beagle (*Lamna ditropis*) should also be noted: the Pacific variety has a wider triangular pectoral; the belly, although remaining white, often has darker patches. The secondary caudal keel is common to both.

The mackerel sharks, which include porbeagles, great white sharks, and makos, are so named not because of their diet but because of the pronounced caudal keel associated with the mackerel family.

COLOUR VARIATION

Although I've never come across one myself, some porbeagles have a defect in body coloration. These fish have a more silvery sheen to their bodies, which is almost metallic. Faint, dark spots cover the body along its full length. Some evidence suggests that these fairly rare captures are more slender in appearance than the average fish.

Specimens have been reported from the Isle of Wight area of the English Channel and off the Cornish coast, where a personal friend, Francis Jones of Abertillery (Gwent, S. Wales), succeeded in landing a spotted porbeagle over 135 kg (300 lbs) in weight. Still in the UK, some porbeagles have been caught commercially off the Shetland Isles, and I have heard a vague reference to a 42-kg (92-lb) fish off the Scilly Isles.

Strangely, there are no records of mis-coloured porbeagles ever being taken in the USA.

I doubt (as some believe) that these are a different species. Fish of all families take on different hues to camouflage themselves when over differing terrain.

SOUTHERN OCEAN RELATIVES

At present, information on two other possible members of the porbeagle family is scarce, and clarification of their true nature difficult to establish. *Lamna whitleyi* and *Lamna phillipi* are found throughout the southern Pacific, including southern Australasian waters, off South Africa, and in South American waters. I have found no reference to these as a rod-and-line sportfish, although reports have been made of commercially caught specimens from the seas bordering the Falklands.

ARE PORBEAGLES DANGEROUS TO HUMAN BEINGS?

There is some evidence to suggest that porbeagles may attack human beings. Several attacks on bathers off the coast of Greece, Israel, Egypt, Italy, and Yugoslavia were certainly perpetrated by porbeagles. Some of these were fatalities — the unfortunate victims carrying the evidence of dislodged teeth. One of the most recent incidents that ended in a fatality took place at San Felice Circeo, south of Rome, during September 1962. A diver, Maurizio Sarra, was spearing groupers when attacked. He died a short while later from his injuries.

In waters surrounding Britain, which are generally cool even in summer, several worrying incidents have taken place. Again, a diver working seawards off the beach at Beesands in Devon in the summer of 1971 was charged twice by a large shark thought to be a porbeagle. This attack is interesting because of the presence of eye witnesses. The witnesses and the unfortunate diver all estimated the shark's length at 4m (12ft). Under the circumstances, this may understandably be an exaggeration; as everyone knows, a fish's size in the water is notoriously difficult to estimate. However, the man was most certainly attacked.

A similar incident took place in the summer of 1982. A diver working rough ground for lobsters underneath Constitution Hill at Aberystwyth in Wales was approached by a large shark. From the description it was almost certainly a porbeagle. The fish made a couple of passes, just having a look, before the diver reached safety. In the same area at Cwm Tdu, during the summer of 1987, a windsurfer was shadowed by a large dark fish. The fish was seen from the cliff tops by the windsurfer's family who, despite all their frantic efforts, failed to alert him to the danger. This occurred at the same time as John Mitchell and myself were taking shark from marks only a few miles away. Fortunately, this can only be regarded as a close encounter as the windsurfer remained unmolested.

On rare occasions, beaches in Hampshire and Cornwall, England, have been patrolled by large sharks that seem reluctant to leave a certain area. Perhaps they are attracted by the constant splash as bathers enjoy the water or perhaps it's nothing more sinister than the presence of baitfish close to shore. Many times, when porbeagles have entered the rubby-dubby slick or chum trail, I've pondered the risk should any crew member fall overboard. This is not being melodramatic, just common sense. In warm water with copious quantities of mackerel blood and pilchard oil about to excite them, this is the most likely time for aggression.

The cooler water surrounding the British Isles, many believe, may inhibit attacks. Certainly in other parts of the world, 18°C (65°F) seems to be a critical lower temperature for shark attack. Sea temperatures rarely reach this in Britain. The attacks in the Mediterranean tend to support this, as water temperatures often exceed 18°C. Most shark attacks on the American coast are attributed to whites and tiger sharks, but some knowledgeable marine scientists feel a few are porbeagles.

THE ORIGINS OF ROD-AND-LINE FISHING FOR PORBEAGLES

The first porbeagles caught on rod and line in Britain were probably landed off Ballycotton in Ireland prior to 1920, when small porbeagle pups up to 39 kg (85 lb) were caught by anglers after pollack. The first serious shark fishing was undertaken by the Marquis of Sligo and Dr O'Donnell Browne. This intrepid pair fished the waters off Achill Island in Co. Mayo (north-west Ireland) and succeeded in taking many fine fish up to 165 kg (365 lb)

from a small canvas-covered coragh. A coragh is a coracle-shaped craft manufactured from thin strips of deal covered in canvas, light enough for one person to carry. The two men were fishing the area back in the late 1920s and 1930s, yet to this day its shark potential remains largely unexplored.

At roughly the same time, two men by the name of Bullen and Herren (who did much exploratory work in Cardigan Bay, Wales) were finding high numbers of porbeagles in their local waters, although the average size could not compare to the Irish fish. American anglers, blessed with such a wide variety of sporting species, tended to eye shark as a nuisance fish and rarely set out to deliberately catch them. However, a painting by Stearns depicts a party of anglers off Long Island, New York, with a shark alongside the boat. Stearns lived between 1810 and 1885, which suggests that sharks were a regular catch even then — many taking baits intended for other fish. Sharks are still, to some extent, regarded by many as a nuisance, but now more and more American anglers fish deliberately for porbeagle as a worthy sporting adversary.

CHAPTER 2

Life-history and Physiology

The first sharks appeared in our oceans during the middle part of the Devonian period, some 350,000 years ago – fish called *Cladoselache*. A rare find in the Cleveland Shales on the south shore of Lake Erie gives us an insight into the beginnings of modern-day sharks: a fossil in an excellent state of preservation representing a fish estimated to be some 1.2–1.8m (4–6ft) in length when alive. In addition to the teeth and fin spines (which are the best structures at retaining their original appearance), the kidney tubules and muscle fibres also remained.

This shark had a torpedo-shaped body, with broad-based, virtually rigid pectoral fins. Also evident are two, low-profiled dorsal fins. The tail structure was heterocercal, akin to modern sharks. Positioned at the base of the tail on each side are small caudal keels – the precursors to the caudal keels evident on the powerful mackerel sharks of today. The mouth was not under-slung as in modern sharks. *Cladoselache* had no opercular gill cover and was doomed to swim forever to maintain movement of water through the five gill slits to the rear of the head. A large eye positioned high up and at the front of the head suggests a fish that was used to working deep. There are no claspers and the assumption drawn from the broad-based pectoral fins is that this was a far-from-fast swimmer with only basic agility. The teeth are interesting because, at the base of the single, high central point, is a small basal cusp at either side. Modern porbeagles have almost identical teeth.

Shark of various types populated the oceans in greater and greater numbers until, by the Cretaceous period, most present-day species had evolved. The first real species of shark was *Palaeospinax*, a small, slim fish, looking a little like a modern spiny dogfish. This shark is the original owner of the under-slung jaw. This jaw was probably protrusible, as one sees it today in the great whites, porbeagles, and many other species of sharks. Between 70 and 100 million years ago, modern sharks appeared much as we see them today, including the Lamnidae. Some physical adjustments have occurred in overall size and dentition, but the shark remains at the top of the food chain – a complete and overpowering predator.

THE SKELETON

Sharks have no bones as such – they rely on a support structure of cartilage. Cartilage is a semi-transparent, very flexible and elastic material consisting of cell spaces formed from a complex protein that encircles a network of connecting tissue-fibres. Zoologists classify bony fish as Osteichthyes and the sharks are known as Chondrichthyes.

Bone creation depends upon cartilage –

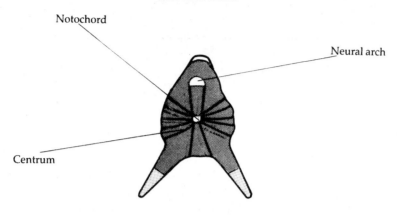

Figure 4. Spinal cord

calcium salts are deposited in the cartilage's core until it becomes brittle and hard, with an almost transparent appearance. At the same time, blood vessels deliver cells (osteoblasts) to create true bone as the cartilage is broken down. As cartilage is a forerunner to bone, cartilaginous sharks were always considered to be primitive creatures, this idea being supported by their early appearance. Anatomical details reinforced this argument, principally the absence of a gill cover or opercular bone and the upward sweep of the spinal column to support the upper tail lobe.

The truth is that the first bony fish evolved some 500 million years ago and the first sharks followed on some 150 million years later, reverting to cartilage — which is lighter than bone and, being more flexible, better suited to a fish of highly predatory nature. There is some bone in sharks, mainly in the skull and in the roots of the teeth, jaw, and fins. A calcification of sorts can also be found in the spinal column.

THE SPINAL COLUMN

The spinal column is constructed of vertebrae. The centrum of the vetebra houses the notochord. Above this lies the neural arch, which provides attachment points for body muscles and provides a route for the spinal cord. Dark areas of calcification can be seen emanating from the centrum.

TAIL AND FIN STRUCTURE

The tail is created and supported by an upward sweep of the spinal column. The upper tail lobe of the porbeagle is slightly longer than the lower. Extra rigidity is achieved by the dermal rays. These are slim, supporting structures housed in the base of the fin; they push out in a simple fan shape. When swimming, the porbeagle propels itself by holding its body almost rigid, using short, strong sideways strokes of the tail for propulsion. These muscular movements pass backwards along the body culminating in thrust at the tail. The muscles themselves are arranged in zigzag vertical blocks along the shark's flanks.

The pectoral and pelvic fins are hydrodynamic. In other words, they force pressure on to the water as a means of steering. When the shark wants an upward lift, the pectoral is raised at the front, tilting to the rear. For a downward movement, the front edge of the pectoral is lowered and the rear lifted.

Many times when watching porbeagles at close quarters in clear water, I've seen them use their pectorals as a means of braking. Tail movement stops, diminishing propulsion, while the pectorals are raised to their maximum. The increase in drag slows the shark. The notch at the rear base of the pectoral gives greater qualities of rotation for just such manoeuvres.

SKIN STRUCTURE

Sharks are abrasive to the touch — they feel like coarse sandpaper when rubbed against the grain towards the head. This is because of the shark's small placoid (plate-shaped) scales or tooth-like structures (denticles). These vary in shape on different parts of the body. Usually, they are shield-shaped on the belly, round on the nose and head, keel-shaped along the flanks, and a sharp-edged diamond shape along the front edges of the fins. Different shapes are required to facilitate movement by cutting drag to a minimum. This is why they lie flat when you rub your hand towards the tail but stand proud when the direction is reversed.

The denticles are constructed from a basal plate that is situated above a cavity of pulp, which is serviced by blood vessels and nerves. Inside the pulp cavity are cells that feed the denture. A thin, hard material (not unlike enamel) protects the denticle's point and outer surface.

TEETH – THEIR CONSTRUCTION AND THE SHARK'S FEEDING TECHNIQUE

The probeagle's teeth are distinctive — they have a sharp point that rises from the root, flanked either side by a single basal cusp. The sharp point is designed for stabbing and puncturing, the small cusps for gripping. The front teeth are the largest, becoming progressively smaller towards the back. They are arranged in a conveyor-belt manner: as a tooth becomes loose and falls free or is lost in an attack, another one moves forward. Five reserve teeth lie angled away from the exposed main front tooth, leading down into the jaw. Tooth replacement probably takes about eight days. Teeth that are beginning to move

Figure 5: The porbeagle's teeth

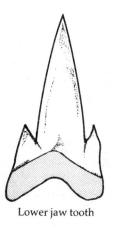

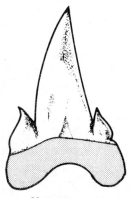

Lower jaw tooth   Upper jaw tooth

outside the line of the mouth are in the process of being shed.

The porbeagle's feeding characteristics are interesting. The shape of their teeth suggests that porbeagles grab and impale their intended prey when it is too large to be swallowed whole. The upper and lower jaws move in opposite directions to drag the meal backwards and into the throat. Sharks cannot chew food – everything is simply swallowed whole. In fact, the word 'swallowed' is misleading: sharks have no throat as such, whatever goes into the mouth goes into the stomach, unless the shark spits it out. The old idea that sharks had to roll to take food is not true. A porbeagle's nose is supple, having muscles that enable it to be raised up out of the way in order for the shark to bite more cleanly. The nose can also be moved from side to side as required.

The jaws are pushed outwards away from the lifting nose at the moment of seizure. This is when the roll *may* be seen. This roll is nothing to do with aiding the bite but more with ease of manoeuvrability. Porbeagles often lift a little in the water before turning to dive deeper again – much like an aeroplane does before going into a steep dive.

DIGESTION

The digestive system is a simple affair. The digestive tract is a short S-shaped tube. The stomach cavity (situated at the end of the oesophagus) is really only an expanse of muscle followed by the S-shaped bend into the intestine, which continues almost directly into the rectum. A spiral valve in the gut provides added surface area for the absorption of nutrients. Tubular glands in the stomach secrete digestive enzymes which – coupled with the secretion of hydrochloric acid by the

gastric glands – breaks food down. Partly digested food travels towards the spiral valve while being continually attacked by enzymes. The spiral valve makes up for the relatively small absorptive area of the intestine, running almost like a spiral staircase along the gut. The suggestion that sharks vomit previously eaten meals during battles with anglers is difficult to evaluate. When gutting sharks there's roughly an even chance of finding the stomach empty or with contents. Some porbeagles I've cleaned have had the small chunks of fish we'd distributed over the side in their stomach (these chunks sink to the bottom and are intended principally to bring the sharks up from the seabed). Larger food items may possibly be disgorged at will by the shark, but I have no personal experience of this.

Even big sharks probably need to feed only occasionally. Low nutritional needs may mean that one good feeding spree can satisfy the shark for several days. Whether the anglers on board a boat who are losing bottom fish being reeled to the surface are losing fish to one persistent shark or several would be an interesting thing to find out. My own feelings are that one shark has taken up station underneath the boat and is picking off what it wants. I would expect a shark to eat approximately 10 per cent of its own weight in one go, and up to 20 per cent over a prolonged feeding period. A 90-kg (200-lb) fish could easily eat 9 kg (20 lb) of fish flesh before abstaining from food.

REPRODUCTION

Males are easily recognized by their two, elongated claspers positioned by their pelvic fin. These claspers lie to the rear during everyday life for reasons of streamlining but, on the point of copulation, they are brought forward to enter the female. Only one clasper enters at a time. (Shark claspers are erectile, as has been proved by experimenting using the hormone adrenaline.)

Porbeagles have not, as far as I am aware, ever been seen actually mating. Being less nimble-bodied, porbeagles may complete intercourse belly to belly, unlike some other shark species (e.g. the dogfish), in which the male coils around the female. Breeding probably takes place at a specific time of year. Most probably in deep water between very late autumn and late winter. It is doubtful if specific breeding grounds exist. I support the theory that a female simply encounters a male at the right time.

Some females I've seen have been very badly scarred across their backs and heads. This is probably the result of males slashing the females across their backs with their teeth during aggressive sexual contact. Of these scarred females, some have been quite small, around the 45-kg (100-lb) mark, whereas I've come across bigger fish, well over 90 kg (200 lbs), that were not scarred. This could support the theory of chance contacts with males. Scars on the dorsal and pectoral fins of females might also be inflicted during the mating process: male sharks may hold the females' fins during courtship, behaviour observed in other species.

Female sharks abstain from feeding when in the nursery grounds; males remain unfed while actually mating. When pregnant, females avoid contact with other females of equal or larger size. Large sharks of both gender are rarely present near small pups.

Porbeagles are ovoviviparous – the fertilized eggs hatch within the womb, develop, and are fully formed when born. The young are therefore able to swim and feed much as an adult would. It is thought that between two and four embryos are present in the early stages of motherhood, feeding on an attached yolk sac. When this is spent, the embryos eat unfertilized eggs and possibly other, smaller embryos, a process known as oophagy.

The smallest porbeagle I've ever come across weighed approximately 10 kg (22 lb) and was found dead on a rocky beach. A friend, John Mitchell of Aberaeron, Mid-Wales, used to run a shark boat from the port and caught on rod and line a small juvenile weighing in the region of 11.5 kg (25 lb). I know of other small pups from the same area, possibly indicating a nursery area close by. A 3-m (10-ft) female caught in the Gulf of Maine (N.E. America) was found to contain an embryo weighing 9 kg (20 lb), probably ready to be born.

RESPIRATION AND CIRCULATION

We have already mentioned that sharks have no opercular bone (gill cover) as do bony fish, which is opened and closed allowing the passage of water through the

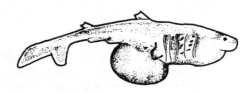

Figure 6: Uterus-resident porbeagle embryo

gills. Instead the porbeagle has five vertical gill slits that allow the flow of water from which the shark draws oxygen. To enable the process to continue, porbeagles must swim forward. If the fish stopped, it would drown. Hence, when a big shark is caught, the best way to kill it is by towing it backwards – water flowing backwards through the gills effectively drowns it. It is doubtful that porbeagles assume a stationary position, taking advantage of moving water currents to obtain oxygen as some other sharks do.

The porbeagle has a heart consisting of the usual four chambers housed down and slightly to the rear of the gills. Blood enters a rearward heart chamber, passing onwards to the upper cavities. These pump the blood into a hollow cavity (ventricle). From here, powerful muscles pump the blood forward into the gills where oxygen intake and carbon dioxide emission take place.

DEPTH CONTROL

Sharks have no swim bladder to fill with air in order to adjust the depth at which they swim. Porbeagles have a specific gravity that is slightly above that of saltwater. Consequently, they have no natural flotation, which means they sink immediately they stop swimming.

Sharks have large livers and it is thought that the oil present in them reduces the fishes' specific gravity, aiding buoyancy. When the liver is large and fat, the shark is healthy; small, thin livers with little oil content are found in injured fish and in males after the mating season.

BRAIN POWER

Anyone who has fought a big shark on rod and line will doubt the words so often associated with sharks – that they only eat, swim, and breed. All sharks are capable of thought and learning, not in the same way as humans but, nevertheless, they are able to reason and retain knowledge. This has been proved by tests in marine laboratories: sharks have been programmed to associate food with certain noises and individual colours. A porbeagle's brain size/body size ratio compares very favourably with those of other creatures, including marine life, birds – even some mammals.

The front segment of the brain houses the olfactory or smell lobes. These receive information from the nostrils as the shark sniffs the water. The mid-section of the brain is concerned with vision and deciphers some of the relayed messages from the sensory organs. The third, back segment controls the body's movement and balance, which are co-ordinated by the incoming pulses received by way of the lateral line.

SENSORY PERCEPTION: THE LATERAL LINE

Water is denser than air. Thus sound travels further and more quickly – in fact, noise travels through water five times more quickly than through air. However, it's unlikely fish hear noise as we do; they probably 'feel' it. Water disturbance created by feeding shoals or the swimming movements of a single fish come to the shark as shock waves. Sharks are aroused far more by an irregular disturbance than a continuous one. If you imagine a wounded fish swimming for a few seconds then resting, followed by a brief attempt at movement, you will appreciate why sharks respond well to irregular shock waves. Low-frequency emissions below 50 Hz have the greatest effect, but signals up to 1,000 Hz induce a response. However, the hit-and-miss pulse is the critical factor.

20

The lateral line runs from the head and along each flank of the body. Further sensors (or ampullae) are positioned around the nose, particularly in front of it, and around the underside of the eye. These ampullae are believed to read small electrical impulses given off by flatfish, etc., buried in the sand. This seems feasible, as one can imagine a shark swimming across the seabed, its nose surveying the ground, monitoring the water by smell and feel.

The ampullae are positioned around a small vial that contains a gelatinous substance in which are small, sensory hairs. This gelatine can be seen oozing from these small pores around the nose a few hours after death. The sensory hairs monitor the passage of water in all directional planes.

It is thought that a shark can detect the earth's magnetic field and, more precisely, the electrical currents set up by tidal movements caused by the prevailing winds. *Lamna* can also detect major ocean currents, in particular the Gulf Stream, as it traces its path across the eastern seaboard of America, across the Atlantic, and breaks to approach and surround the British Isles.

As a shark swims (continuously passing through the earth's magnetic field) it creates its own electrical field that varies in voltage as the shark alters its compass heading. It is thus entirely feasible that the porbeagle can navigate using the earth's magnetic field.

VISION

Porbeagles have a relatively large eye, suggestive of time spent swimming deep where light levels are low. The eye itself is a simple round circle with no noticeable pupil — the characteristic dead eye of the shark, totally expressionless. Sharks can distinguish colour but this may be for unusual reasons. Sharks kept in marine tanks develop the ability to distinguish red from white. What may be happening here is that a sight-by-silhouette pattern has emerged. Red is the first colour to fade underwater, becoming black. It may be that a shark's eyes perceive surrounding seawater as a lighter tone, while any dense mass of food or baitfish appears darker at depth.

That being so, when I have used balloons to suspend hook-and-line baits at a certain depth, I've noticed that the porbeagles that cruise up the chum trail with their dorsals out of the water seem to be fascinated with the brighter yellow and white balloons. They often pass by darker blues and reds. Perhaps sharks see colour on the surface, black and white tones taking over when swimming deep.

Sight appears to play a minor role in feeding, only useful in the last metre or so before a food item is taken. North-east American waters and European seas are rarely clear for any distance. Even at a shallow depth, visibility is unlikely to be more than a metre or so. Winds, storms, and natural ocean movement keep particles of sediment in suspension at all times — turbidity is a fact of life. Sight is therefore the least effective sensory organ in these waters, but the shark does have a mechanism to make the most of the available light. To help them in clouded water, sharks have a reflective layer of tiny silver plates behind the retina, the tapeta lucidum. Light that has already passed through the retina is reflected back again onto the light-sensitive cells, doubling the light and hence the image seen by the eye.

SMELL

Smell is the second most important sense for a feeding shark. A wounded fish is sensed by the shark's lateral line, which

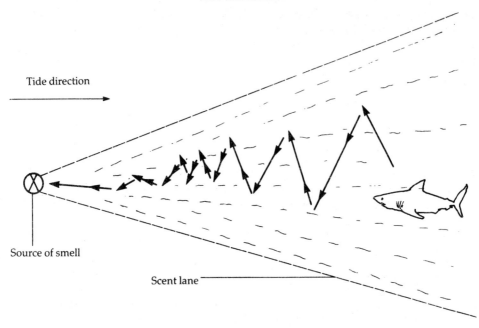

Tide direction

Source of smell

Scent lane

Figure 7: Swimming pattern of food-seeking porbeagle

gives it a bearing on the fish. The shark approaches in a straight line and at a moderate pace until the scent is picked up. Scent is then followed until visual contact.

Sharks can smell blood at a one part per million dilution. They follow the scent by swimming in a crossways action. Should the shark lose the scent, it will swim in a wide circle until the scent lane is relocated. As the scent begins to concentrate, the shark moves more quickly, swinging its head from side to side to maintain contact with the strongest scent trail. This head movement ceases the moment the shark sees its prey. A powerful burst of strokes from its tail carries the shark the last metre or so.

The nostril on *Lamna* is on the upper jaw in front of the eye, almost in line with the leading edge of the mouth. The nostril has two tubes, one for the intake of water and the other to release it. Water passes over the olfactory sacs for evaluation, and is then emitted from the exit tube.

PARASITES

Unlike some sharks, I have not seen porbeagles accompanied by cleaner-fish. However, they do suffer from the occasional parasite. Prominent amongst these is a minute sealouse, *Lepeophtheirus*. These have a round head and an elongated, tube-like body that culminates in a long, whip-like tail. They attach themselves to the skin, usually on the forward edge of the tail and at the base, where they form little clusters. I have occasionally found them singly on the leading edge of the dorsal. If you look closely at a cluster of these parasites, you can see small white circles on the shark's skin. This, I assume, is the telltale scar left after one of the pests has fallen away — the discoloration caused by the feeding action of the parasite. I have never come across any infestation in the gut cavity or the gills, although I have heard of diseases in the liver and abdominal tract.

22

CHAPTER 3

Distribution Worldwide

The North Atlantic porbeagle (*Lamna nasus*) and the Pacific porbeagle (*Lamna ditropis*) are sharks of temperate seas. Temperature tolerance of the species varies between 4°C (40°F) and 20°C (67°F). The North Atlantic porbeagle frequents the eastern coast of America, from Cape Hatteras in the south to Sandwich Bay in Labrador, Canada. This area includes the Gulf of St Lawrence and continues as far as the southern tip of Greenland, across the top of Iceland, dissecting the Norwegian Basin to Murmansk in the Barents Sea off Russia. This delineates the northern

Figure 8: Territory of the North American porbeagle (Lamna nasus)

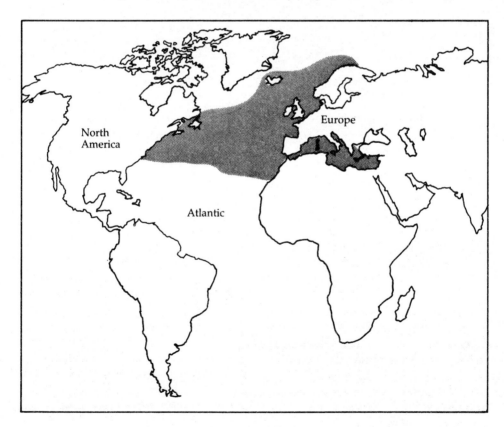

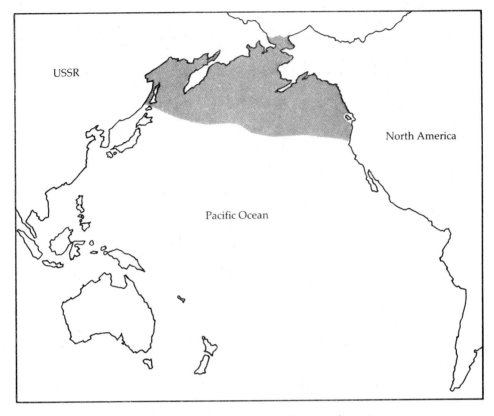

Figure 9: Territory of the Pacific porbeagle (Lamna ditropis)

frontier of the porbeagle's terrain.

From Murmansk, down the coast of Norway, and into the North Sea there are porbeagles. The seas around the British Isles have major concentrations, as have the Bay of Biscay and the whole of the Mediterranean save for the upper Aegean and Black Sea. Their territory extends south in the Atlantic as far as the shores of Morocco.

The Pacific porbeagle inhabits the North Pacific from roughly Cape Disappointment on the western seaboard of America, through the Bering Sea, and penetrating the Sea of Okhotsk, Russia. The preferred temperature range is again 4°C (40°F) to 20°C (67°F) maximum.

In the following discussion I shall concentrate on the Atlantic porbeagle's habitat, but most of the information regarding the type of terrain, etc. is also applicable to the Pacific porbeagle.

THE BRITISH ISLES

The South
The Isle of Wight porbeagle fishing grounds were made famous in the late 1960s when Dick Downes and Trevor Prince returned to port with many large shark – the best weighing 147 kg (324 lb), at that time a British record. Further exploratory work followed during the early 1970s, resulting in the opening up of the fabulous ground that lies to the south-west of the island. A very deep, under-sea trench comes within 2 miles

(3.25km) of the shore as far as St Catherine's Point. At its greatest depth it reaches 55m (30fm), yet the borders of the trench lay only 22m (12fm) down. The deepest western end culminates in huge pinnacles of rock standing proud of the seabed, known locally as 'the overfalls'. In a storm this is a seething mass of foam and spray, with huge swells. Even with no wind and relatively calm seas it is still a wild place, carrying indistinct patterns of swells and white water. The number of sharks caught on rod and line here seems to have fallen in the ensuing years, but commercial catches from the general area have proved that some fish still remain. This decline may be part of *Lamna*'s life-cycle: one area is popular for a few seasons, then the fish move on.

The coast of Devon and Cornwall has seen countless battles with big sharks and will continue to do so. One of the best-known centres is Padstow in Cornwall. Shark-angling started here in the early post-war period with Group Captain Pat Lombard in the boat *Bounty*, along with Tommy Morrissey in the *Girl Maureen*. Fishing mainly for blue shark, they still took porbeagles, which sowed the seeds for others to follow.

To the north of Padstow lies a small rocky headland called Cambeak, near Crackington Haven. Water depth can be as little as 25ft (7.5m) over rough, jagged ground and, consequently, many fish are lost. Some massive fish have been seen and hooked here. Those successfully boated have included the current British record of 211 kg (465 lb) by Jorge Potier in 1976 and Derek Runnel's 208-kg (458-lb) fish in the following summer. The same area has other good marks around Trevose Head and Tintagel. However, though their ground features are similar and fish hunt there, they do not occur in the numbers associated with Cambeak. Many of the fish hooked come from the inshore, shallower water, only a half mile or so from shore. This is true of other areas as well.

Porbeagles are undoubtedly responsible for chopping fish off anglers lines over the numerous wrecks in the upper English Channel off Kent and Sussex. Many longlines have been damaged by big fish that take up to a dozen hooks off the line – original bait, hooked fish, and all. Some porbeagles (mainly pups) stay attached to prove the point. Sightings of fins by commercial and pleasure craft were an almost daily occurrence in the upper Solent during the 1950s, although no one took up the challenge.

The Scilly Isles and the Channel Islands also have the makings of prime fishing. A few fish have already been taken, but far larger fish exist. A shark estimated to be 3m (10ft) repeatedly took small pollack and wrasse off anglers' hooks whilst cruising along the breakwater in the Isle of Alderney. The length was estimated and identification was made by reliable sea-going people. A porbeagle tagged off Jersey turned up only one month later off Muquies Plateau in France. A 27-kg (59-lb) fish, again tagged off Jersey, was retaken two years later off the Isle of Wight.

Wales

Cardigan Bay in Wales has also seen its share of sharking, going back over fifty years. However, it took until 4 July 1989 to see the first fish over 90 kg (200 lb) caught. Other, bigger fish have again been hooked and lost and, undoubtedly, more will come from this area in due course. The three main ports actively involved in shark fishing are Newquay, Aberystwyth, and Aberdovey. At Newquay, sharks are taken mainly over clean ground in a moderate depth of water. There are several wrecks to the south of Newquay and when these are exploited to the full for general bottom fish, anglers and skippers persistently trying for shark in this vicinity will do well.

A few miles north lies Aberystwyth, home of the largest charter fleet on the whole Welsh coast. In the main, sharking from Aberystwyth requires a fair amount of steaming before the grounds are reached – some 10 miles (16km) or more offshore. Aberystwyth has a good potential for future catches, especially when you look beyond the 20-mile (30-km) barrier where good ground features suggest even better results.

The little port of Aberdovey is home to Wales's most famous sharking boat, the *Ceffyl Mor*, which is skippered by a lifelong friend of mine, Charlie Bartlett of Tywyn. It was aboard the *Ceffyl Mor* that I was fortunate enough to land that first, Welsh 90-kg (200-lb) fish. The ground out of Aberdovey has a rocky reef that gives way at a moderate depth to fairly clean sand. Most fish are taken close to shore; large fish are certainly present, being regularly sighted and hooked.

Though sharking began in earnest some seventy years ago, even in Britain the potential for further productive ground has hardly been explored. The Welsh side of the Bristol Channel round to Milford Haven has seen a few pups boated to about 45 kg (100 lb). A serious effort here by good anglers who understand sharks would yield some excellent results. The wrecks that lie in the mouth of the Bristol Channel and south to Minehead, Somerset, hold porbeagle. All the charter skippers report incidents of bottom fish being chopped when reeled to the surface.

In North Wales, the Isle of Anglesey is surrounded by deep water, and fins have been seen and small porbeagles have been caught in inshore nets. A 36-kg (80-lb) fish was taken in a net set 450m (500yd) out off Dinas Dinlle beach in North Wales during the summer of 1986. Porbeagle have been reported inside the Menai

Straits – in fact, the museum in Liverpool has one.

Scotland and the North

Fish have been caught in the waters off the Mull of Galloway in Scotland, yet little exploration has taken place. Again, the ground features and depth look superb. Stories abound of massive fish hooked on longlines aboard boats and dinghies fishing the whole of the west coast of Scotland. These battles are short-lived – the fish breaking away, or the anglers cutting the line. There are few charter boats and the weather is bad for long periods, but huge fish are waiting to be caught.

Some notion of the possibilities can be gleaned from recent shark catches around the Shetland Isles. A small group of dedicated anglers began fishing the waters out from Lerwick in the late 1970s, taking fish between 86 kg (190 lb) and 204 kg (450 lb). A shark in the over 227-kg (500-lb category was also seen close to the boat. Shark were there again during November 1987, when fish up to 116 kg (256 lb) were taken well to the south of the island.

The North Sea contains an untapped fishery of sharks. Over the past years, so many sightings and contacts have been made it's surprising no one has tried to learn about their movements and preferences. During the 1950s there were several examples of porbeagles taken in nets and longlines set off the Norfolk coast, and by small trawlers working out of Great Yarmouth. In 1960–3, netters working the Yorkshire coast off Whitby took several fish to the local fish-markets. In October 1961, the angling writer, Harry Tallant, saw a shark he estimated to be 4m (12ft) in length on the surface under Hunstanton Pier (Norfolk). The shark was thought to be a porbeagle.

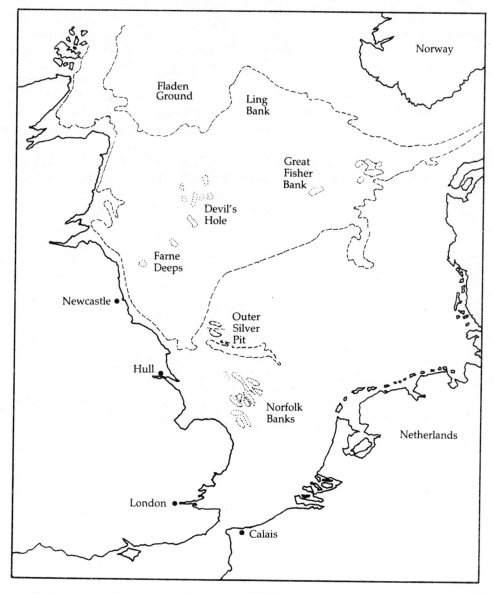

Figure 10: The North Sea

During 1964, three porbeagles were caught by netters 7 miles (11km) off Amble in Northumberland. The largest fish was 2.5m (8ft) long and would have weighed in the region of 160 kg (350 lb). This particular fish was sold to a fishmonger in Edinburgh fish-market. The significant thing about it was that it was taken in December when the principal food source would be whitefish and herring. Shark have also been observed in the mouths of several of the major estuaries, including the Firth of Tay and the Firth of Forth.

Porbeagles on the main offshore fishing grounds of the North Sea have long been known by accidental commercial captures. However, fewer catch reports have been forthcoming lately because of over-fishing in the North Sea over the past few decades. By looking at the relevant Admiralty charts of the North Sea, and allowing for food-support systems, sharks should be present in good numbers over the Norfolk Banks off the Norfolk coast, off the Humber coast in the Silver Spit area, the Farne Deeps north of Newcastle, and as far north as Aberdeen in Scotland. These areas should offer good fishing well into the autumn. The winter and weather permitting, sharks must also be resident in the more stable depths of Fladen Ground off the north-east coast of Scotland.

Ireland

Ireland is the shark anglers' idea of heaven. Deep water and rough ground cover almost the whole of the Irish coast. However, apart from the early fish taken by the Marquis of Sligo and Dr O'Donnell Browne, sharking in Ireland hasn't yet been fully developed — although I've a feeling the door will soon be opened.

Most Irish shark-fishing concentrates on the blue shark, which likes warmer water than the porbeagle and occurs off the south and west coasts. Porbeagle are also present in these waters, probably in greater numbers than is realized. During the summer of 1989, a companion, Colin Albert, and myself undertook a trip to Castlehaven in Co. Cork. I wanted to assess the blue-shark potential (which was superb), but also found evidence of large porbeagles. The very first day a porbeagle herded mackerel round the boat. It would not take one of our baits, being far more interested in the shoaling mackerel. However, it did pass within a few feet of the boat on its first pass, and I estimated

the length to be between 2.7 and 3m (9 and 10ft). Its weight was probably in excess of 200 kg (450 lbs). I also experienced a run on a 1.8-kg (4-lb) pollack bait set at 18m (60ft) in a total depth of water exceeding 50m (155ft). By the attitude of run and the chewed remains of the bait I'd reeled in, I am almost certain this was a porbeagle.

This incident occurred close to the Stag Rocks that lie off Toe Head. The Stags are perfect porbeagle ground, having a surface that shows rock falling rapidly to 34m (110ft). On a spring tide in the sound between Toe Head and the Stags, the tidal run exceeds 4km/h (2kn). From Castlehaven round the Fastnet Rock and on to the edge of Bantry Bay is the area I would most like to target for a prolonged expedition in search of the massive porbeagles I know are there.

Irish rod-caught fish of note have been taken at Dungarvan (Co. Waterford), Kinsale (Co. Cork), Liscannor (Co. Clare), Galway Bay, Galway, and Keem Bay (which is part of Achill Island where those early fish came from). Porbeagles have been reported in many other areas by both commercial landings and rod-and-line contact. In particular, I suspect big shark are present off Killybegs (Co. Donegal), where hooked fish are lost on a regular basis. The south side of the Aran Islands (Co. Clare) and around Great Blasket Island (Co. Kerry) also seem good. I would also propose the Causeway coast, especially Rathlin Island (Co. Antrim), where fast tide-rips create the conditions porbeagles like the best. Commercial captures again provide evidence of existing stocks all the way down the Irish east coast, where fish are available both winter and summer.

Commercial activity also suggests that the very largest sharks lie off the west coast in the open Atlantic. Porbeagles over 3m (10ft) and weighing 318 kg (700 lb) and over have been taken on long-lines and in herring trawls 50–100 miles (80–160km) out off the north-west coast over the Rockall Rise, which is a deep, subterranean mountain range.

EUROPE

Leaving British shores and heading south, we see a similar pattern of recorded captures, both commercial and rod-and-line. Porbeagles are frequently taken on floating longlines set for broad-bill swordfish in the southern quarter of the Bay of Biscay and off the Portuguese coast, as well as in the usual nets. Evidence for the southward movement of some fish comes from the case of a fish tagged off Falmouth, Cornwall, England, and recaptured almost two years later off San Sebastian in Spain. A heavy concentration of porbeagles can be found in the waters off La Coruna, N.W. Spain. This is over a major subterranean rise that is part of Cape Finisterre, and porbeagles can be found further south, near the edge of the Iberian Basin. There are no particular hotspots in the Mediterranean, the sharks appearing to be fairly evenly spread because of more stable food supplies.

USA

Montauk on Long Island has long been associated with catches of porbeagles. These shark show with some consistency throughout the summer months. Offshore, major concentrations are found over the Grand Banks to the point of the Flemish Cap. Note the occurrence once more of under-sea mountain sructures. Between Long Island (New York) and St John's (Newfoundland) there is an overlap of food: big shoals of both mackerel and herring mass, which keep the sharks in concentrated numbers. There seems to be a designated route for these porbeagles, from the tip of the Flemish Cap across the Reykjanes Ridge to Iceland. *Lamna* is found in good numbers in the vicinity of the ridge, but numbers subside rapidly the further north you head.

Porbeagles have the habit of winter accumulation in areas of concentrated whitefish shoals, particularly cod. A particularly heavily populated area occurs off the north-east coast of America between Nantucket Sound and the Gulf of St Lawrence.

MIGRATION AND FEEDING AREAS

Shark are present in the waters off the Norwegian coast all year round, and there is a definite migration of porbeagles from south to north. A porbeagle tagged off the Jersey coast was caught over two years later off the Danish coast. However, a marked increase in numbers is apparent during the mid-winter period. Commercial whitefish trawls have produced porbeagles exceeding 270 kg (600 lb) in January and February. One of these was once again a tagged fish. It was particularly interesting because of the time lapse before recapture. This porbeagle was tagged off Jersey in the summer of 1973 and turned up thirteen years later in February off the Lofoten Islands in Norway. Its weight at the time of recapture was 160 kg (350 lb). These winter fish – together with the travel pattern of autumn, commercially caught fish up the North Sea and around the top of Scotland – suggest a definite northward migration by some sharks as winter approaches.

The sprat also holds the sharks' attention during the colder months when dense shoals gather well offshore. An inward movement of these sprat shoals during calm, autumnal weather may keep some porbeagles within range well into

November – even in shallow water. However, a short spell of cold frosts usually sees the sprat shoals reversing their course, taking the sharks with them.

As we've seen, the porbeagle is a pan-oceanic shark, well capable of adjusting (at certain times of the year) to varied locations as dictated by food supply. In the winter they can be found far offshore where water temperatures are more constant and the baitfish shoals are concentrated. However, this is only half-true for, when deep water lies close inshore and food is plentiful, sharks will also be present.

With the coming of spring they move into shallower water, hunting over clean sand and broken ground, but they are chiefly attracted by rocks. Hence, the prime marks are where hard, jagged, rock pinnacles fall vertically to the seabed. Substantial under-sea rock projections carry an enormous and fairly constant supply of food – find that food source and you've found your shark.

A second attraction of rocks is the element of surprise. Consider the speed and manoeuvrability of the porbeagle and you will realize how superbly equipped they are for a surprise attack on any food fish. It's easy to imagine a shark casually swimming around a slab of rock at the base of a reef coming across a pollack that bolts for cover. A burst of speed from the shark's tail and it's the end for that pollack.

Where two such reefs are in close proximity, there is probably some pattern of change-over – the porbeagles alternating between the two by a defined route. Locating this route can give the angler opportunities for remarkable sport. These routes are mostly found along the trenches that run between two reefs, areas of rough ground, or where sandbanks and gravel beds give deeper lanes for them to follow. If there is more broken ground along their path, they may hunt across this if the tide is suitable for feeding. They tend to position themselves just off the bottom on flat, rough ground and between mid-water

Figure 11: Route of porbeagle along shallow sandbank and deeper gully

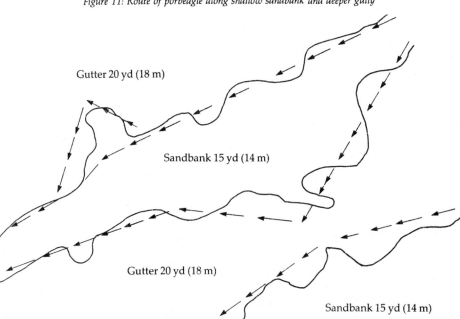

Gutter 20 yd (18 m)

Sandbank 15 yd (14 m)

Gutter 20 yd (18 m)

Sandbank 15 yd (14 m)

and the surface when over clean ground. This is possibly for reasons of camouflage: their backs are dark, so when they are on the seabed over a rocky bottom they are unlikely to be seen. In mid-water and above, food fish below them will only see the pale belly of the shark against the lighter-coloured surface reflection.

In water less than 20m (70ft) deep, and over a sandy bed, aim to find a deeper ridge or bank that travels some distance; porbeagles tend to swim above these following the contours of the gully or bank. When a run of tide crosses a rocky reef they have a habit of being just inside the outer edge of the run-off, moving back inside as the tide eases. The points of reefs and exposed headlands have eddies on the downtide side as the tide races past. These hold the shark while the flow is strongest.

Such places see a concentration of food fish as many get swept into the eddy to be picked off by shark.

If the reef is a large one with vertical slabs of rock rising 50ft (15m) or more from the seabed, they stay on the side the tide hits first, working the lower reaches and only rising in the water when the tidal flow falls away.

Early and late in the season, most of their feeding is done on the seabed and in the lower levels where food is concentrated because of the stable temperatures. At these times, the substantial areas of sandbanks and, again, rough ground (where cod, whiting, and pollack can be found) hold the key to the best locations.

The sounds or channels between the mainland and islands or two separate

Figure 12: Position of porbeagles between headland and island, and between two islands

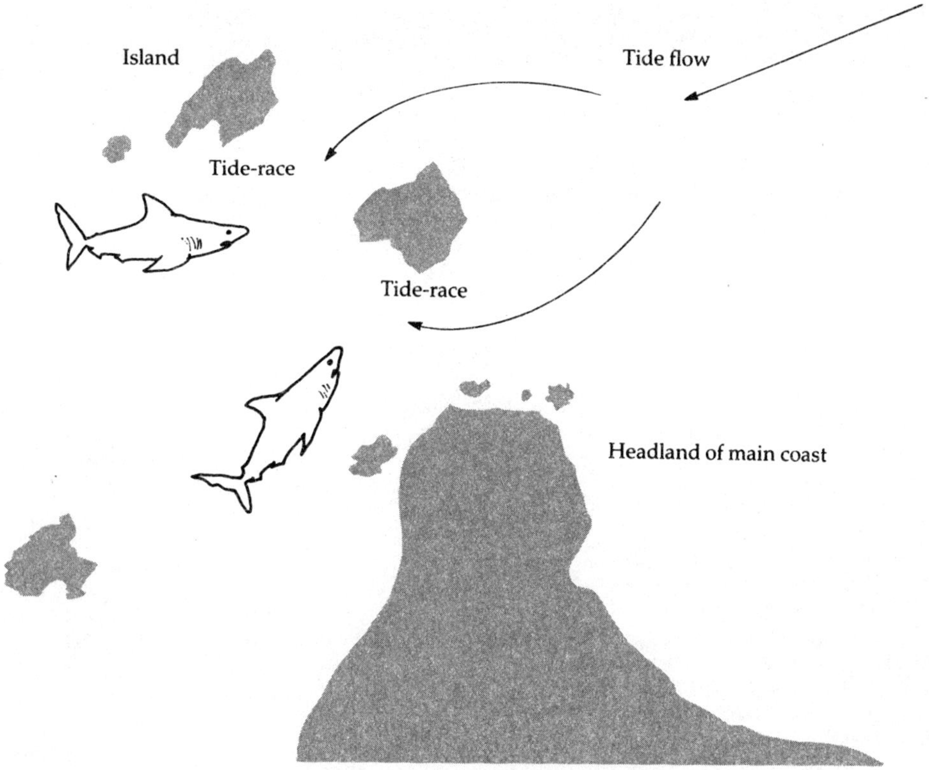

31

Figure 13a: *When a fast tide crosses over a relatively shallow reef porbeagles will take advantage of the slacker water to be found on the down-tide edge. Here numerous eddies and overfalls will concentrate small food fish that get swept along by the tide, creating an easy food supply. A large eddy will be found at the very end of the reef created by the passing tide run. Here, concentrated baitfish will again draw porbeagles. As the tide run eases, the shark will revert to the opposite side of the reef that faces the tide.*

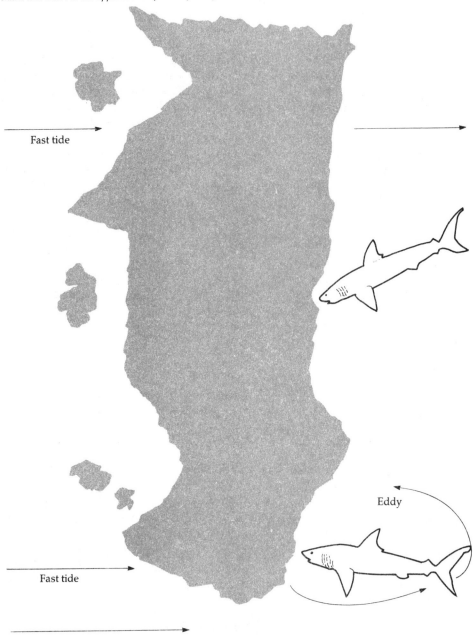

Fast tide

Fast tide

Eddy

Sharks on outside of reef

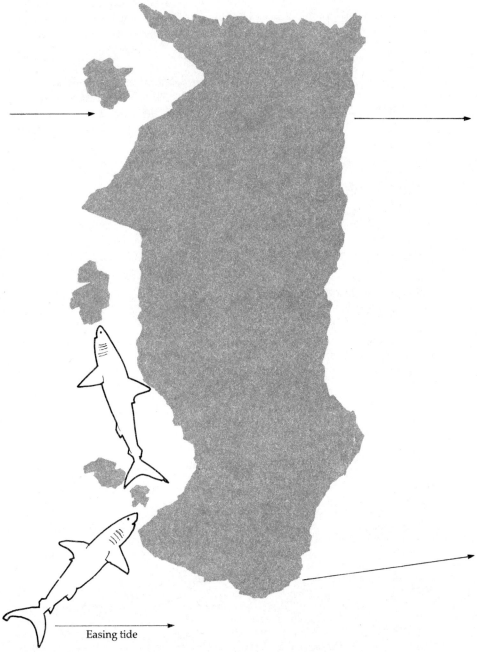

Easing tide

Sharks move back inside reef

Surface

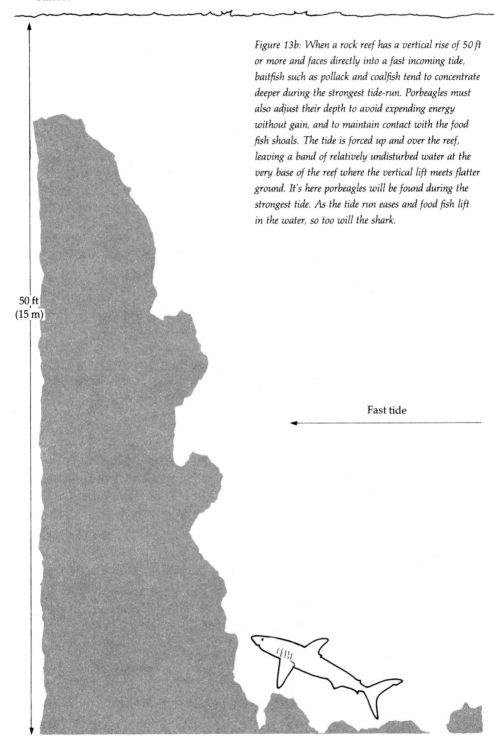

Figure 13b: When a rock reef has a vertical rise of 50 ft or more and faces directly into a fast incoming tide, baitfish such as pollack and coalfish tend to concentrate deeper during the strongest tide-run. Porbeagles must also adjust their depth to avoid expending energy without gain, and to maintain contact with the food fish shoals. The tide is forced up and over the reef, leaving a band of relatively undisturbed water at the very base of the reef where the vertical lift meets flatter ground. It's here porbeagles will be found during the strongest tide. As the tide run eases and food fish lift in the water, so too will the shark.

50 ft
(15 m)

Fast tide

Surface

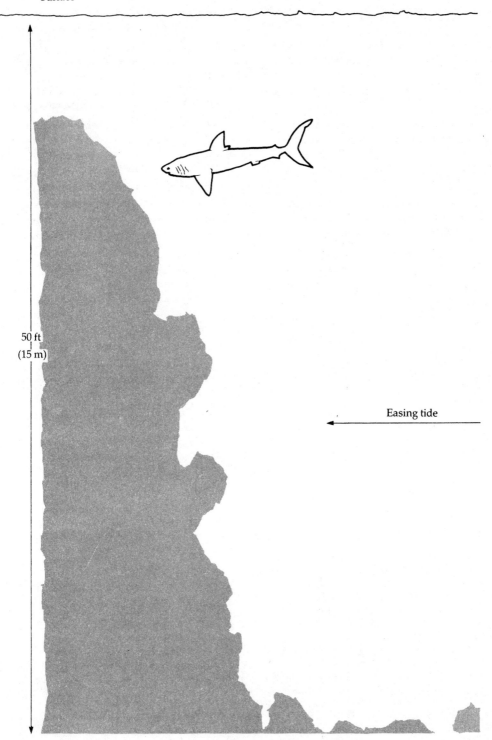

50 ft
(15 m)

Easing tide

islands, which carry a strong current, are likely to hold porbeagles. In such places they will stay deep when the tide is strong and rise towards the surface as the flow eases. Again such places hold a concentration of food fish.

Above all, remember that porbeagles love to swim alongside rock. Bear this in mind when shoal fish such as mackerel are scarce. They adopt the tactic of following the borders of rough and clean sand, relying on the element of surprise to gain a meal.

Deep wrecks hold the attention of big sharks. Porbeagles are opportunists and realize that the high population of fish housed in and around a wreck will keep them well fed. The reason wrecks are little

explored at the moment is that most lie in deep water where tides are fierce and anchoring is only possible on the smallest neap tides. Any sort of tide-run restricts drifting time to too short a period on the bigger tides, when shark are more likely to be feeding. These shark are mostly positioned in mid-water, working the baitfish shoals, or at the level of the wreck's superstructure, right on top of the wreck's residents.

I'm convinced some shark become territorial for short periods over wrecks. A certain wreck will witness the persistent chopping-off of hooked fish until weather patterns change or food supplies fall away. When anglers return to the wreck, the shark has usually gone.

CHAPTER 4

Tides, Currents, Temperature and Weather Patterns

TIDES

Like any other fish, porbeagles are ruled by the tides. When feeding inshore their preference is for the bigger tides that create movement in the water. There seems to be a chain reaction − all fish seem slow and feed less for shorter periods during neap tides. Sharks, as predators, hunt when peak activity occurs. This may also explain their feeding bursts followed by periods of abstinence. Fish feeding on neap tides may also have been unable to find enough food over the spring-tide.

As a general rule, to be successful in neap tides it's important to be well off-shore and in a good depth of water. My observations over the past ten years indicate a definite outward movement of the majority of sharks, away from the inshore waters of less than 18m (60ft) on neaps. A precise timing is impossible, but when the tides reduce to less than their middle scale of height, shark runs become less likely. This is not always true in areas that experience massive tidal push and where current speed can be measured at 9 km/h (5kn) or more. These areas may only yield shark on the lowest neaps.

Offshore over deep water, tides become almost immaterial. I've taken shark from several areas 40 miles (64km) offshore during the lowest neap tides. Tide size and size of shark has no correlation − both large and small fish can be expected on

any size of tide. It's impossible to set ground rules for these things, but you're more likely to encounter small groups of porbeagles feeding loosely together during neap tides. However, when fishing well out, sharks come in singles with definite periods between their runs. The reverse is true when fishing shallower water close to the shore during a spring-tide period: food fish are plentiful, and so are the incoming shark. A dozen runs in a day is quite feasible.

Each area has a different pattern of feeding and movement, depending on local topographical features. A small bay with deeper water close in can fish well on the flood tide when small baitfish are forced into the bay by the tidal current and become bottled up. Access to deep water is essential, yet you may only need to be half a mile from the shore to find fish. This type of terrain occurs, for example, in Ireland, the north-west and north of Scotland, and the Cornish coast.

Some reefs only fish on the flood tide when a strong tidal push is deflected at a right angle to hold back the food fish. Other reefs peak during the ebb when several conflicting currents converge and supercharge the available power. This type of situation can be found where large estuaries enter the sea − their outward-flowing currents can be traced several miles out from land by the change of water colour and by the weed lines. Sharks will continue to feed after the flood tide has died if you can locate them in a deep trench where a fresh ebb-tide crosses.

OCEAN CURRENTS

Understanding the relevant main ocean currents is helpful, as porbeagles appear to congregate where two or more different currents converge. The most important current in the North Atlantic is the Gulf Stream. This carries warm water across the ocean and alters sea temperatures around the British Isles and parts of the European coast, giving them a milder climate.

The Gulf Stream begins in the Caribbean off the north coast of Cuba. It flows north through the Straits of Florida and across the under-sea mass of the Blake

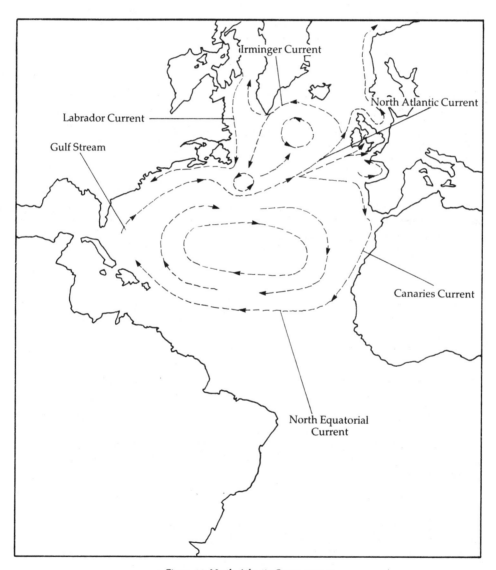

Figure 14: North Atlantic Ocean currents

Plateau. In the vicinity of Delaware bay, the northward flowing Gulf Stream (which can travel at 9km/h–5kn) is forced outward by the final weakening finger of the colder Labrador Current that travels north to south from Newfoundland.

Off Cape Hatteras, the Gulf Stream's path can reach down over 1,000m (3,000ft) with a bottom width of up to 40 miles (64km). Further north, the flow becomes less stable and controlled and is pushed east. The mass of water breaks up, forming large rings of warm water that can approach 150 miles (240km) in diameter and that can achieve distances of 60 miles (96km) a day. These travel in clockwise and anticlockwise directions, eventually reforming with the original core. The eddies to the north of the main flow rotate clockwise, while the eddies to the south of the flow turn anticlockwise. The northern rings have a core of warm water, the southern rings a core of cooler water. Weaker rings (called mesoscale eddies) also occur, attaining distances of 15 miles (24km) a day.

Porbeagles favour the edges of the circles, where movement is evident. Few enter the dead water found in the centre. This may also be a result of temperature:

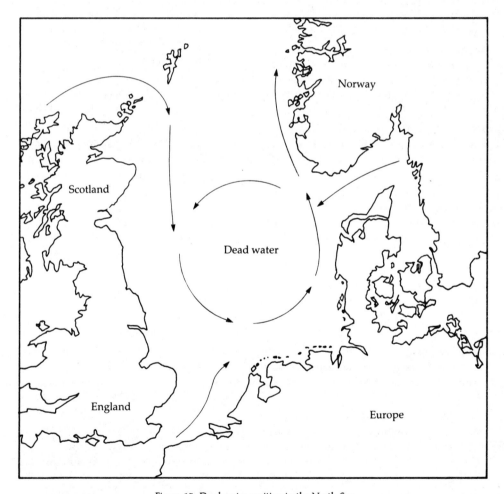

Figure 15: Dead water position in the North Sea

the water at the edge of the circles mixes with cooler water and is hence probably more attractive to sharks as the currents carry more food.

When these break-ups occur over the Grand Banks off Newfoundland, the westerly air-stream that blows across them meets both the warm waters from the Caribbean and the cool waters of the Labrador Current. These sudden changes in temperature create the huge fog banks associated with this region. The Labrador Current also pushes icebergs into the North Atlantic. (It was this combination of weather and tides that sank the *Titanic* in 1912.) And it is this mixing of two currents that gives the Long Island to Newfoundland coast such a reputation for porbeagles.

Over the Grand Banks, the Gulf Stream becomes the North Atlantic Current, which splits three ways. The northern branch (the Irminger Current) flows around Iceland. The central and strongest core bathes the British Isles in warmer water, continuing right to the heart of the Barents Sea. The southern flow becomes the Canaries Current. This touches the whole of the French coast, down to the mouth of the Mediterranean, and on – going full circle to re-enter the Caribbean Sea.

The North Atlantic Current passes close inshore between the Shetland Islands and the coast of Scotland, travelling south into the North Sea. Other fingers push in to the English Channel and the Irish Sea. In the Bay of Biscay the circulation of current is anticlockwise. Again, this creates dead water on a large scale, and the greatest number of porbeagles will be close to shore where the current is moving. This same problem may occur in the North Sea. Here some circulatory effect may create dead water over the area between the Greater Fisher Bank in the south and the Ling Bank to the north.

With this in mind we can see why big porbeagles have been taken off the north-west of Ireland 50 miles (80km) out. This area is in the direct path of the North Atlantic Current. Another stem hits the coast of Cornwall around Padstow and leads up the English Channel to touch the Isle of Wight. A finer finger enters Cardigan Bay in Wales. Those commercially caught porbeagles along the east coast of England and Scotland were right in the middle of the main flow of the southward-spilling current. So were the tagged fish recaught in Norwegian waters, and the commercial kills made in that area as well.

LOCALIZED WATER TEMPERATURE

Water temperature affects the way in which porbeagles feed and is therefore a guide to their location. Few British anglers bother to take temperature readings while shark-fishing, yet in the United States and parts of southern Europe where gamefish are sought, having a precise knowledge of the water's temperature and its changes is an essential part of any trip. Video depth-sounders now more often include the facility for water temperatures to be read out at differing depths. This is invaluable in finding fish.

Submerging a standard thermometer a few inches under the surface serves the purpose, but do this on the sunny side of the boat – even this can make a difference in the read-out. Remember, if you submerge the thermometer to a deep pressure it will break the glass. The strongest thermometers are the type used in milk production. Putting a bucket over the side is fine, but if the bucket has been in the sun and collected heat prior to submersion this will alter the reading. When taking temperatures, submerge the gauge for sixty seconds (no longer) and keep your fingers well away from the mercury.

Any moving water creates heat, however marginal: during the colder periods, the odd porbeagle may be found by locating a warmer moving current in an otherwise featureless sea. Surface water also catches and holds the heat of the sun, although this retention diminishes the deeper you go. The upper, warm layer is called the epilimnion. The mass of colder water that hugs the seabed is called the hypolimnion. These waters do not mix – they are separated by a narrow band of water that is subject to rapid changes in temperature – the thermocline.

During the summer months, porbeagles tend to stay above the band of action in the thermocline. They swim in mid-water and above. This applies to the offshore deeps where depths approach and exceed 30m (100ft). In shallower water, which is subject to more mixing through storms and irregularities on the seabed, water temperature is more uniform. Here some bottom feeding will be noted, especially during rougher periods of weather. The Atlantic is warmest in September and the early part of October. American waters can expect a high of around 20°C (67°F), while Britain's seas top out at around 16°C (60°F). The Bay of Biscay may reach a degree or so higher.

As the autumnal change manifests itself, the surface waters cool and sink deeper. This process continues until a balance of temperature occurs. This is only a partial balance as the surface will be fractionally cooler and deep under-sea currents can introduce colder water at base level. By mid-winter, the stable, constant-temperature water rests in the lower layers; the surface layers are subjected to rapid and uncomfortable change. In winter, por-

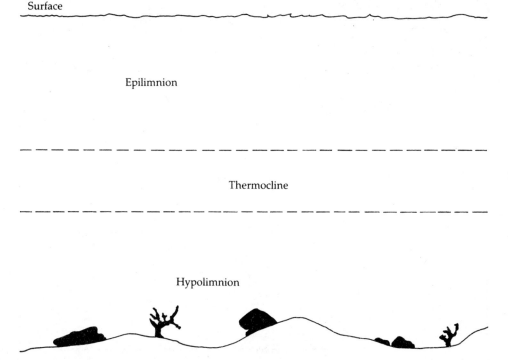

Figure 16: Segregation of warm and cold water by the thermocline

beagles do most of their feeding in the depths, rarely rising above mid-water.

Shark anglers looking for early-spring fish would be well advised to fish their baits very deep or on the bottom in deepish water, leaving the shallow areas until the end of April and onwards. The exact time will depend on the severity of the winter. Few frosts and little snow keep water temperatures higher than normal, encouraging an early return. A hard winter may delay the sharks' coming by as much as six weeks.

Thermocline action appears to be most prominent around deep, rocky reefs. In my many conversations with divers I have learnt that when an onshore wind pushes a flooding tide against a deep reef that lies in the direct path of the two, warm water collects along the upper reef and pushes

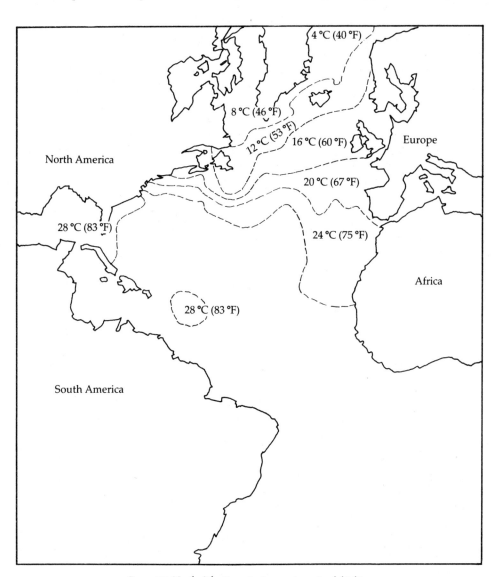

Figure 17: North Atlantic water temperatures (peak high)

downward at an angle – forcing cooler water into a narrow band at the bottom. Divers feel the change in temperature each time they pass through the thermocline. This may explain why some reef fish, such as pollack, suddenly change feeding depth as tides ebb and flow. Sharks must also adapt to this change to stay with their intended food source.

An observation of my own is that of thermocline action against a static current. Imagine a current of water flowing south-westward. With a wind from the west, warm water is pushed up against this current and piles up. The thermocline will fall deeper as it nears the current. Porbeagles tend to find this phenomenon and stay in it until the tide changes and the current and thermocline disappear and normalize. The surface water of the moving current always gives a cooler reading than the build-up.

The colour of seawater gives an indication as to whether it's warm or cold. Black water, with no clarity, is cold. I have never experienced good fishing of any description in black water. Grey water means a higher temperature, and this increases as the sea takes on a green tinge and gains a little clarity. Warm water is clear and blue, although at times plankton blooms create some discoloration.

The northern end of Cardigan Bay in Wales is a prime example of this. The inshore waters are fed by three major river estuaries, and a large eddy is evident in its northern quarter that holds dead water. The blue-water line is well away from the land – some 24 miles (39km) during cooler weather periods. In settled conditions, you cross the blue-water line only 10 miles (16km) out. During the very settled summers of 1976 and 1989, this line could be found only 6 miles (10km) out. The edge of the blue-water line is always a good place either to drift or to set a pattern of balloon baits.

Currents that carry warmer temperatures can also be found by the presence of weed lines. The weed that floats from estuaries and beaches during stormy periods is collected and held by currents to form a long line of demarcation. Notice in the vicinity of weed lines or the usual collection of offshore flotsam and jetsam a change in water colour – usually from a greenish-grey to a green shade of blue. This is the warmer water and the most likely place for a porbeagle because of the presence of baitfish. You will notice that small areas of the sea are devoid of jellyfish and others will be full of them. Again, large numbers of jellyfish indicate warmer water and are well worth investigation. If mackerel are difficult to find, their presence is often indicated by jellyfish.

FEEDING DEPTH

Looking back through my fishing log has helped me to assess the likeliest temperatures and the likeliest level sharks are apt to feed. During hot spells, when surface temperatures are over 15°C (60°F), porbeagles can become lazy and moody, especially when the sea is like glass. Any feeding fish are probably between 10 and 20ft (3 and 6m) down. Some fish will show themselves on the surface at such times, fins out of the water and slowly swimming up the slick of chum. I've read that once these fish dive you are guaranteed a take. This is untrue: at best there's a fifty-fifty chance of acceptance. I often find that this is the last you will see of them – as already suggested, these fish are moody.

There are days when several shark can be seen swimming around, up to the boat and ignoring all baits. This is most evident from late June onwards to September, when the surface begins to cool. In water less than 15°C (60°F), the bulk of fish will be between 7.5 and 13.5m (25 and 45ft)

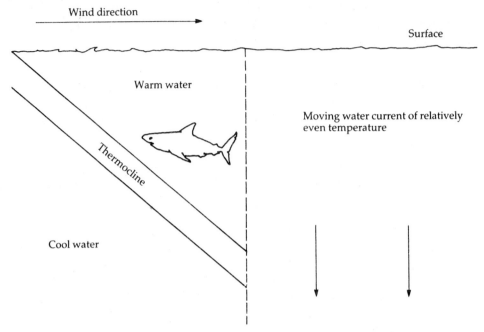

Figure 18: Position of thermocline when tide and wind are in opposing angles

down. Cooler than 12°C (54°F) and they will be under the thermocline or on the seabed in the shallower zones. Surprisingly, when temperatures exceed 16°C (61°F) they move offshore into water deeper than 80ft (25m), where temperatures stabilize. This behaviour is also associated with mackerel (a principal food fish of the porbeagle). Mackerel shoals break up and move out during prolonged periods of fine, hot weather.

Their moving out of warmer water may be due to the porbeagle and mackerel being warm-blooded (see Chapter 2). If their body temperature is higher than the surrounding water, they may feel uncomfortable, and seek out greater depth where the water is cooler. Always bear this in mind when setting the depth of your bait. I also believe that the largest porbeagles will be found in colder water for the self-same reason.

WEATHER PATTERNS

During periods of calm weather, water clarity is increased as the sea carries less suspended sediment. Such conditions are obviously the least favourable for feeding shark. Light penetrates to some 4.5–6m (15–20ft) and then filters out quickly. In these conditions, the porbeagle uses its camouflage to work underneath baitfish shoals, rising to intercept them.

When even a light breeze takes the glare off the water, the infiltration of light falls and feeding activity increases. This is apparent when a sunny day becomes hazy or, better still, cloudy. The previously idle shark suddenly feed with intent. The best days of all are when cloud cover comes at evening in conjunction with a newly flooding tide. Dull days with fine drizzle are also good. Shark can again be seen on the surface, generally feeding well when the tides are suitable. Days of heavy rain are less reliable. Fish can be caught but seem less inclined to committed feeding. Perhaps the rain hitting the sea's surface disrupts the shark's sensory organs and send them much deeper.

Porbeagles feed best on a falling barometer when a blow or storm is approaching. Feeding activity is also observed as the barometer rises again. Very high barometric pressure puts them off feeding.

Some wind is an advantage: porbeagles feed with the wind. If the wind and tide travel the same way, conditions are favourable. The more the wind leaves the angle of the tide, the less they seem to feed. A local wind is not always needed to put life into the sea. A storm several hundred miles away can be felt in local waters by a heaving swell. These swells encourage otherwise lazy shark to hunt for food. Big storms that persist for several days will scatter the shark, taking them away from the inshore shallows and into deeper water.

When extreme high temperatures stabilize for some time, the sea can experience a severe explosion of algae. Just such an event occurred in the waters off southwest England and off the coast of Wales during the summer of 1989. Anglers on the American coast are also familiar with the presence of such blooms. These blooms are massive collections of microscopic life-forms. They drift with the ocean currents and, when conditions are favourable, form huge, dense blankets of colour on the sea's surface. Two large areas of white-coloured bloom appear off the coast of Iceland and over the Rockall Bank each year, with varying density. Plankton dies in huge numbers, sinking to the seabed. The bacteria that live in the depths cannot consume the numerous corpses fast enough. The resulting decay causes deoxygenation, and the effect is that fish (and porbeagles) move out, leaving a barren void.

These blooms can be several colours — white, green, yellow, and the infamous orange or red tide. In some places orange or red bloom is called the tide of death or May water. It was the red tide that entered British waters in 1989; fishing became poor and anglers and charter skippers had to search the sea for areas of relatively clean water to find some sport.

The severity of the red tide, and its possible future implications, can be measured from the events of 1987 and 1988 on the east coast of America. Dead dolphins were washed ashore on the beaches of New Jersey in June 1987. Their bodies were covered in lesions, and many were so badly decomposed that pathological evidence from tissue samples was of no value. Also evident were signs of skin disease and viral and bacterial infection.

It was subsequently found that whales off Canada and north-east America had died through contact with a poison excreted by algae in those north-eastern waters. This had been passed down the food chain to the whales via mackerel. The toxin collected in the gut of the baitfish and was transferred, after accumulation, when the mackerel was eaten. The dolphin, which eats the menhaden (a member of the herring family) suffered in much the same way.

In the spring, the menhaden migrate northwards into the porbeagle's territory. The consequences are obvious, but porbeagle corpses are unlikely to be found as they would sink to the seabed the moment the shark ceased to swim. Fortunately, storms break up these blooms and baitfish (and porbeagles) are quick to return.

CHAPTER 5

Baits and Baitfish

MACKEREL

Mackerel are probably the angler's most important baitfish, and perhaps the porbeagle's too. It's not surprising that mackerel inhabit identical water to *Lamna*. Mackerel are present along the entire north-eastern seaboard of America, with particular concentrations off Long Island and in the Gulf of St Lawrence, but few are found in the waters off the northern coast of Newfoundland.

The whole of the British Isles is surrounded by mackerel, and there are well-favoured areas off the south-west corner of Devon and Cornwall, the Irish Sea, the North Sea, and up the coast of Yorkshire into Scottish waters. Mackerel are also found throughout the Bay of Biscay, off the coast of Spain and Portugal, and they also feature in catches throughout the Mediterranean. The Norwegian coast sees a fair run of these fish during the summer months.

The mackerel is a pelagic fish, feeding mainly between mid- and surface waters in depths greater than 30m (100ft), but they are frequently found on the seabed in water less than 20m (70ft) deep. No ground feature seems particularly desirable, but they do favour the tide-runs at the edge of rocky points or reefs. Any place (usually a tidal eddy) that collects and holds smaller baitfish will attract mackerel.

They move inshore during late May or early June in dense shoals, feeding mainly on small baitfish. They continue this habit until the middle to end of October, when they revert to a demersal habit (bottom dwelling) moving out to deeper water for the winter and taking the bulk of the shark with them. During the winter they live in huge shoals that hug the seabed in deep, stable water, which undoubtedly holds the attention of numbers of porbeagles. Spawning takes place in April to June when the shoals break up into smaller groups and move inshore, bringing the sharks with them. ·

Mackerel not only provide the bait for our hooks but must also make the chum that brings the sharks to those baits. This means we must be able to catch mackerel efficiently. Strings of four or six feathers or, better still, silver-tinsel-type lures are worked in the water by lowering and lifting the rod tip. This works very well when the shoals are dense: an hour's good feathering will provide enough for the day's needs. Instead of a lead weight to sink the feathers, use a piece of chromed tubing filled with lead and armed with a small, treble hook. This proves to be good at attracting mackerel to the feathers.

When the shoals are thinly spread it may be necessary to troll the feathers behind the boat at speeds of around 3.5km/h (2kn) until the mackerel are located. A useful tip is to have a length of rope (smallish in diameter) with feathered snoods attached at relevant distances over, say, 8m (25ft). A good weight of about 1 kg (2 lb) keeps the feathers down. Don't make the snoods too long or frequent tangles will ensue. This can be worked all day if necessary to keep fresh bait coming aboard or use two, trolled steadily behind the boat, for multiple catches when bulk numbers are needed for chum.

Mackerel tend to be deeper during bright sunny days and nearer the surface during overcast conditions. They adjust their depth in accordance with the tides and the filtration of light, often being higher in the water on flood tides and lower during ebb tides – though this is a loose description. The best feeding times are the first of the new flood for four hours and the similar period on the ebb. Also favourable are dawn and dusk.

HERRING

Herring (*Clupea herangus*) are another prime food source of porbeagles. Their colouring is bluish-green on the back with bright-silver sides. Small patches of irridescent blue and green may sometimes be observed just to the rear of the gills. The gill covers and flanks may be shot with a gold or reddish tint. Their average size is about 25cm (10in), but they may attain 43cm (17in) and 0.7kg ($1\frac{1}{2}$ lb) in weight.

There are major fisheries for herring off northern Europe and into the Barents Sea. The once-famous herring fishery of the North Sea, where abundant catches were an everyday occurrence, is now a shadow of its former self. However, fair numbers can still be found, and their main spawning areas are situated off the north Norfolk coast, in the upper English Channel, and off the coast of Scotland.

The herring's southern zone penetrates as far south as Spain but does not include the Mediterranean. Herring are found all the way across the North Atlantic, including the waters around Iceland and the southern tip of Greenland. There are major fisheries between Boston in the USA northwards to Cape Race in New-foundland.

Herring can be divided into two distinct breeding groups: some are spring spawners, shedding their eggs in shallow inshore waters, whereas others prefer the late summer and autumn period, well off-shore on the edges of tidal paths and under-sea banks.

Herring make a vertical drop by day to a depth that can exceed 300m (1,000ft), but rise again by night to the surface, following the plankton upon which they feed. Herring can be seen feeding in the surface film on bright moonlit nights. It is also said that heavy frosts encourage these fish to boil on the surface.

Herring were once located by what was called the Herring's Telephone. This was a series of thin, long wires lowered by the fishermen into the depths. The fish's movements would catch the wires, which could then be felt. This gives some indication of how dense the mass of these shoals can be. Porbeagles have been known to contain as many as forty herrings when gutted – all perfectly whole – but with the telltale puncture marks of those pointed teeth.

Herring can also be caught on jigged feathers, but the actual size of the hooks the lures are tied on needs to be reduced to a size 2. Silver lures outfish all others. Small trout flies, with some silver content, can be very effective when worked in teams of four or six.

POLLACK

What British and American anglers refer to as pollack are in fact two different fish.

*Figure 19a: The pollack (*Pollachius/Gadus pollachius*)*

The American pollack is actually the same species as the British coalfish, which is dealt with in the next section.

Pollack (*Pollachius pollachius*) are lovers of deep rocky waters where fast tides rip through. Their colouring is varied: the back is usually a dark brown or green, shading to pale green and yellow on the sides, with a white belly. When resident near kelp-infested rock, they can be a gold or bronze colour with splashes of green and red. The lateral line has a pronounced curve just above the rearward tip of the pectoral fin.

Pollack abound around the British and Irish coasts, across the North Sea and up as far as the Barents Sea. A thin line drawn across from the Shetlands to Iceland marks their most northerly home, while all the coast of France, Portugal, and Spain – as well as the upper coastal belt of the Mediterranean as far as Sicily and including Corsica – hold pollack. This species is not found on the American side of the Atlantic.

Pollack are rarely caught in sufficient numbers to feed the chum trail, but they do make excellent bait and are the principal attraction for porbeagles hunting rough ground and rocky reefs. Pollack are also prevalent over deep-water wrecks. Peak numbers occur inshore during summer and autumn. Wrecks come into their own during the winter months. Spawning takes place during the spring in water about 225m (750ft) deep. The first pollack appear back on the inshore reefs in late April and, predictably, so do the first porbeagles.

Feathering is again the best method for catching pollack when numbers are required quickly, but the feathers should be larger than those used for mackerel. Good colours are white and red, although silver is also effective. Pollack up to 2.2 kg (5 lb) can be used for bait, and these tend to sort out the biggest shark.

COALFISH

The American pollack is the British coalfish (*Pollachius virens*). A coalfish can be identified by its straight lateral line and the sharp points to the tail fin. The true pollack's tail fin is square, cut and the lateral line curved. Coalfish are a dark green or black on the back, with olive sides and a white belly.

The coalfish has a more northerly range of habitat than the pollack, being found north of Iceland and penetrating the Barents Sea as far as the coast of Novaya Zemlya, an island off Russia. They range over the whole of the UK and Ireland and south to southern France. They are also found around the southern tip of Greenland, along the whole of the Canadian coast from Cape Chidley in Labrador to Long Island, New York. Like pollack, coalfish are lovers of rough rocky ground. During the winter months small coalies can be found close to shore, but the larger adults rarely come into water less than 18m (60ft) deep. The colder months see them in depths of over 30m (100ft), making them a prime food source for porbeagles. Spawning takes place between January and May, before migration.

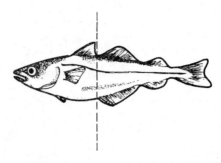

Figure 19b: The coalfish (Gadus/Pollachius virens) (The broken line shows the difference in dorsal and pectoral fin alignment between pollack and coalfish)

Coalfish as bait lack the scent of oily fish, but porbeagles seem to have no trouble in locating them. They are most effective when used over or in the vicinity of rough ground where the shark expect to find them. They are particularly good as a ledgered bait placed at the junction of sand and stone. Coalfish in the 1–2 kg (2–4 lb) bracket are ideal. These fish are also prevalent over deep-water wrecks, conforming to a similar pattern to that of pollack. Coalfish are strong and tough, making them an energetic livebait that provide plenty of movement for the sharks to home in on.

PILCHARD

Primarily found from the Mediterranean as far as the upper North Sea, the pilchard (*Sardina pilchardus*) – a member of the herring family – is rarely associated with the porbeagle. This is an oversight, for porbeagles frequently appeared amidst the boats that fished for pilchard off the coast of Cornwall. This industry has now largely gone, but fair catches are sometimes taken from the English Channel and North Sea.

Porbeagles have only infrequent opportunity to feed on these fish in northern waters, when suitably warm temperatures prevail. The northerly migration of the pilchard occurs after spawning ends during mid-summer, when the dense shoals edge closer to shore.

The pilchard is herring-shaped, but it has larger, easily removed scales and a rounder body. The back is a blueish-green turning to gold on the sides, with a silvery or white belly. It attains a length of around 25cm (10in).

There are major fisheries in the Bay of Biscay and off Portugal, where they are canned as sardines. Porbeagles commercially caught in these areas have been found – as one would expect – to have fed almost exclusively on pilchards.

SPRAT

Although the sprat (*Sprattus sprattus*) rarely reaches a length exceeding 15cm (6in), its abundance in shoals attracts porbeagles. The sprat occupies almost exactly the same locations as the porbeagle on both sides of the Atlantic. A dark-green back shades to bright silver at the sides. Some splash of gold may be observed around the gill covers.

The adult sprat tends to frequent waters over 45m (150ft) in depth during the summer months but goes deeper with the onset of winter. They will rise to the surface like herring at night as they follow the rise of the plankton. A late run of porbeagle accompany the sprat shoals off the Devon and Cornish coasts during the mid-autumn period.

OTHER BAITFISH

During the colder months when porbeagle feed deep, white fish form a major part of their diet. The cod (*Gadus morrhua*) covers the same territory as the shark. Cod are present in waters as varied as the surf of open beaches to depths approaching 545m (1,800ft). In deep water they tend to feed in shoals, well off the bottom but below the thermocline. Cod feed extensively on herring and capelin, and they will sit underneath the mackerel shoals taking any stragglers. This sums up why I set such store by – and draw the reader's attention to – having knowledge of the habits of baitfish and their movements. Even if the actual shoal of baitfish carries little interest for the shark, the presence of smaller predators feeding on the smaller fish, will. Understanding the food chain is vital to success.

Whiting (*Merlangius merlangus*) are a species I regularly find in porbeagles' stomachs, particularly in the early season and when you catch them close to the bottom in deeper water. Some pre-occupation with whiting is evident (as you would expect) when they are abundant. Black bream (*Spondyliosoma cantharus*), confined to the Mediterranean and as far north as the southern half of Britain, are lovers of those rocky reefs and, being shoalfish, attract shark. They are lively fish with excited body movements that make them an ideal livebait.

Caught porbeagles have been found to contain all the above species, along with small conger eels, ling, dogfish, gurnards, garfish, and flatfish. Anglers who have hooked rays have lost them to shark, and it's logical that, when rays swim off the bottom (which they do occasionally) they become part of the shark's diet.

Salmon are also on the menu. Salmon are vulnerable both when close to shore prior to entering rivers and when they make their way to the rich feeding grounds as far afield as the Norwegian Sea. The Pacific porbeagle's diet consists to a great extent of salmon that run into the great rivers of western America and Canada. Evidence of porbeagles present in the vicinity of salmon comes from many examples of shark being caught in – and damaging – equipment designed to capture salmon.

The capelin is another small baitfish that, when located, may indicate the presence of feeding sharks. This applies mainly to the American angler. It is found mainly in the region encompassing the Gulf of St Lawrence and north to Labrador, and the whole inshore region of Iceland as well as the upper Norwegian coast. It rarely exceeds 23cm (9in) but masses in huge shoals attracting smaller predators and sharks.

Porbeagle undoubtedly take garfish and skippers as they swim in the surface layers amid the chum trail. I've never actually seen a porbeagle take a garfish, but I have noted garfish leaping frantically from the water and, within a few minutes, a shark run on the deadbaits has developed. This has occurred too often to be a coincidence.

Another significant factor is the rise of plankton and baitfish to the surface layers at night. I've tried on several occasions to catch shark at night using similar tactics as one would by day. However, this was an elementary mistake. Knowing that the food source rises in the water as night falls, it follows that the shark must do the same. It's interesting to note that many commercially set lines are at a depth of only 2.5m (8ft) and are fished through the night. The swordfish fishermen of Portugal take many porbeagle in this manner when after the big billfish.

Squid could be the key to the porbeagle's presence in the surface layers at night. Squid can be seen on the surface attracted by the bright lights of fishing trawlers, etc. It's equally likely that on bright, moonlit nights the same thing happens. Squid have phosphorescent particles under their skin, and these glow at night and may well be a visual attraction for shark. This is the basic theory of those Portuguese fishermen: billfish feed on squid at night and so it's safe to assume that the porbeagle does as well — as the commercial catches suggest. Deeper-fished deadbaits are well below the night-time feeding band.

The best way to secure squid baits is by the light method. Bright lights of over 250w placed just above the surface will bring them up. You can either scoop them up in a big land net or gaff them — although this damages them and defeats the real purpose. Some anglers employ heavy jigs festooned with hooks but, again, it rips the body tissue. You can keep them alive by placing them in a bait tank that allows the passage of water as the boat is moving or, as a makeshift tank, use a 2.5 l (5 gal) plastic drum, weighted at the bottom and drilled with small holes. Watch the ink when handling squid; it's not dangerous, but stains badly. Three species of cephalopods (squid, octopus, and cuttlefish) prove useful as a free-lined bait, being drifted away from the boat and then slowly retrieved.

The cephalopods can be stored as a convenience bait on ice. Prolonged submersing in water (which should be changed frequently) removes the staining ink. For prolonged freezing, pack them individually: never put several in one bag. Only use fresh squid — the flesh should be white and odourless, any pinkish colouring suggests a bait well past its best.

Fish not normally thought of as shark bait may be eaten, provided they are presented in an acceptable way. John Mitchell of Aberaeron in W. Wales experienced runs on whole, farmed trout of 1.4 kg (3 lb) in weight, and a friend caught a small pup

of 32 kg (70 lb), on a freshwater chub. This works when large, natural baits are scarce, but I've more confidence in natural baits.

Frozen baits are surprisingly effective. Both mackerel and herring freeze well but, again, fish intended for actual hook baits need to be packed separately in plastic bags with most of the air removed to decrease the chance of freezer burn. Try to get intended baits back to the freezer as soon as possible after capture, preferably by keeping them alive in a bait tank or keeping them on ice. Use only the fast-freeze section of your freezer. Make sure the bait is fully thawed before placing the hook, to avoid poor presentation.

FIND THE BAITFISH, FIND THE SHARK

Most people will have realized how important this chapter is. The pattern of a porbeagle's life is directly linked to the baitfish just described.

The first shark arrive on the deep rocky reefs at the end of April when the first pollack arrive. The biggest numbers come when the mackerel move inshore during June, guaranteeing a prolific food supply. As the mackerel break up as autumn closes, herring are there to fill the gap. It's a constant cycle: the most successful angler will be the one who taps into the shark's grapevine and makes an educated guess as to where they will be and what food will predominate. Perhaps the worst time of all for sharking is the mid-summer period: shoals of baitfish are dense and widely spread, and this causes the shark to scatter over a huge area, making their location difficult. A thoughtful angler stands a better chance early and late in the year, when food is scarcer and the shark are therefore inevitably concentrated in smaller, defined areas.

I'm also a believer in matching the bait to what the shark are feeding on. I'm sure when one species is plentiful porbeagles become pre-occupied, leaving less available baits alone. All baits should be as fresh as possible – preferably caught on the way to the shark grounds. Many believe sharks are dirty feeders that eat anything. This could not be further from the truth. As a predator designed to eliminate the weak, they are used to eating live fish they catch themselves or fish chunks that fall to the seabed from the carnage above. Fish that sit in the sun or lie in a fish box on deck lose much of their natural smell. The blood also congeals, which restricts those essential trickles of fresh blood leaking into the tide.

CHAPTER 6

Chum or Scent Trails

The Americans call it chum; in Britain it's rubby-dubby. Whatever you choose to call it, it's the best means of bringing porbeagles to the boat and within striking distance of your baits. The original idea of using trails of minced fish for shark to follow and to become excited by came from America at the turn of this century when the pioneers of modern shark- and game-fishing found they achieved increased catches using this method. British anglers, taking those first tentative steps towards pioneering the UK's waters, were quick to recognize the effectiveness of putting scent in the sea.

The best fish for creating chum are the oily fish, such as mackerel, herrings, pilchards, etc. – and they don't need to be fresh, unlike hook baits. In fact, the older the chum fish are (within reason), the better. It's a never-changing fact that the more effort you put into angling, the greater your rewards will be. This applies three fold when it comes to the dubby. The more smell you release from the stern, and the bigger the area you cover, the greater becomes your chances of pulling shark into the scent lane.

Obviously, to begin with you need plenty of baitfish. It's best to feather these the day before a shark trip. Aim to have around 300 $\frac{1}{4}$-kg ($\frac{1}{2}$-lb) fish at your disposal. Leave these in a plastic fish box, covered by something that deters seagulls but allows the passage of air. It is all the better if the day is hot and humid – oily fish tend to deteriorate rapidly, and that is just what you want.

On returning to port, the by-now (we hope) high fish should be minced or pounded to mush. There are two ways to achieve this necessary fine mush. A large cast-iron mincer with a handle is the usual tool. This should be bolted to a static structure or, better still, to a small wooden table bolted to the deck. On more trips than I care to remember I've been trying to feed the fish into the mincer, turn the handle, and stop the whole unit sliding about at the same time. Having another crew member add their weight to the mincer doesn't really help. I now prefer to fillet the fish removing the backbone but leaving the fillets attached to the head. Removing the backbone avoids a build-up and eventual clogging of the mincer by the fine bones. Feed the fish in head first: if the tail fillet goes in first the broader head will jam and cause a blockage. The resultant paste should be placed in a bucket.

When the bucket is just under half full add bran – the same as is fed to animals. Use only good-quality, fine bran, not the cheap stuff that has all manner of coarse, hard bits in it. This is mixed like kneading bread. Aim for a dry, stiff mixture that holds its shape.

The third and last ingredient is pilchard oil. You can buy this in small bottles but it works out very expensive. It's far better to purchase it in bulk. Add about four tablespoons to the bucket and remix. Mix enough overall to fill the average rubbish can three-quarters full: fill it to the top and you'll regret it.

Bran serves two purposes: first, it stiffens the fish paste, second (and more importantly), it soaks up all the natural juices and oils. As the bran soaks this up it swells and increases in volume by about one-quarter. Fill the rubbish can to the top and the swelling bran will flow over. Leave the mix overnight with the lid on.

I now use emulsifiers when creating chum. Emulsifier, in the form of sodium laurel sulphate, helps to break up the oil content more quickly and effectively widens the avenue of smell. At the same-time, the smell value is slightly weakened. To mix this solution, work to a formulae of 78.8 per cent seawater and 0.2 per cent sodium laurel sulphate. Stir this well, adding the final 20 per cent of neat pilchard oil. Do this slowly and stir the whole liquid frequently. I add about a coffee-cup full of this to a bucket of chum.

A further additive of interest are amino acids. These need to be very carefully used as too strong a solution will actually deter fish, not attract them – according to tests done by marine scientists. The best mix, I find, is about 20 parts per million. I use 35 ml of amino acids mixed with 1 l (2 pt) of seawater. I further dilute 150 ml ($\frac{1}{4}$ pt) of this with another 1 l (2 pt) of seawater. This gives a value factor of a little less than 20 parts per million.

Amino acids are effective only over short periods. In cool water they are released very slowly – in fact, too slowly to be effective. The higher the water temperature, the quicker the release that occurs, with a short (but effective) attraction value. They can be added to a drier-than-normal chum mix or dripped in as a separate agent to concentrate the amino acids in the centre of the scent lane. A word of warning: there is some doubt as to the overall safety of amino acids. Until the situation is clarified, wear rubber gloves and do all your mixing outside to avoid inhalation.

The best containers for holding dubby are fine-weave onion-type bags. These are strong, but allow a free flow of water in and out to carry away scent. These should be placed one on each stern post, with the last quarter of the bag submerged. In rougher weather, it may be necesary to put one bag inside another – this allows more of the bag to remain in contact with the water and yet not wash out the contents too quickly. In addition, I like to place a third bag up by the bow where the scent lane will divide, travelling with the tide either side of the stern. This effectively widens the scent avenue. Give the bag a good shake every ten to fifteen minutes to give the trail a little boost of smell and bits.

I like to cut some whole baitfish into chunks and have this just touching the water at the stern; this adds liquid blood to the water. Another good system is to make a soup, either by mixing minced fish with seawater or by placing some fresh mackerel or whatever in a bucket and adding water. As they loose blood, the water becomes a strong-smelling solution. A clean 5-l (1-gal) can with two small holes pierced in the base holds the soup, the can being hung over the gunnel adding fresh blood to the slick. I favour this method while actually travelling to the shark grounds. Hang two cans of the soup just over the edge of the gunnel and the constant drip of blood leaves a weak (but definite) invitation for the shark to follow. Some crew members on major boats are given the job of ladling this soup over the side as the boat is moving. This is a tiresome task, and I find the soup-can method more efficient.

54

In the early part of the year, it's useful to put dubby down with the anchor. Vegetable bags are no good for this as predators with teeth will obviously eat straight through them, releasing the contents. Make a metal mesh box some 45cm by 30cm by 30cm (18in by 12in by 12in). The bag goes in this and the metal box does not hamper the retrieval of the anchor to any noticeable degree.

How does the scent trail or slick work? When the scent trail is in full flood, the oil will sit on the surface with any broken-up bits of fish and bran sinking through mid-water. The smell lane will follow the tide, but the oil slick at the surface will (to some extent) follow the drift of the surface wind.

I always feel more confident when I cut some baitfish into 2cm by 2cm (1in by 1in) cubes and add these sparingly to the slick, say, one every minute. These gradually sink to the bottom and roll away from the boat. These will lift any sharks that are swimming on the seabed. Don't overdo it or you will feed the sharks as opposed to attracting their interest. In the same way, watch that other anglers don't throw any large fish bits over inadvertently. Some anglers use sawdust instead of bran to save money. This is a false economy, because it just doesn't work nearly as well. When baitfish are scarce, you can get away with a straight mix of bran and pilchard oil. This does work, particularly on blue shark and, to a lesser degree, on porbeagles.

When on a trip lasting for several days, the livers from any kept shark should be added to the chum. As discussed in Chapter 2, the livers have a very high oil content and seem to attract other shark like moths to a lantern. The livers should be put through the mincer and used in the next fresh bag of dubby.

It's an old wives' tale that sharks' livers and blood added to the tide puts other sharks off the feed or keeps them from approaching the boat – instead, this is one of the biggest assets you can have. Many boat captains deliberately leave the body of a freshly killed shark hanging from a stern post to help add that blood. I've noticed that this often brings the sharks much closer to the boat, and their usual shy nature fades – they become more aggressive and show off. Watch the dubby bags when this happens, for they are prone to attacking the bags. I've seen them with their heads completely out of the water, coming determinedly after the bag when it is being lifted clear.

I like to add a couple of fresh bags of dubby as the day goes on to pep up the smell. It may be that once the smell is stable, a weakening of the scent value would not discourage the shark from following the trail – but why risk it? Keep that smell as strong as possible right up until it's time to leave.

Dubby has a secondary use, in that it also attracts other, smaller fish. All this activity helps lure the shark. Often, when mackerel have been scarce, the chum trail has brought enough for fresh bait and for dubby for several days.

The use of animal blood for porbeagles does not work. I've tried ox blood, chickens' blood, and pigs' blood. They seem to repel the shark, for I've yet to have a run when using these foul additives. I no longer bother, and I'm glad they are ineffective as they are distasteful substances, doing more harm to the sea than good. Never throw old chum away at the end of the day and never re-mix it with the new as this weakens the scent. It is better to break it into hand-sized chunks and add it at intervals as cloud bait. This can be done the following day; it sinks to the bottom breaking up as it does so.

Shark skipper, Paul Yates of Newquay in Wales, is always thinking of better ways to catch shark. He came up with a superb method for mincing fish, which provides a finer mix and is much quicker to prepare.

Paul uses 45cm (18ins) of stainless-steel tube some 15cm (6ins) in diameter with a T-shaped handle fastened to the top. This is worked vertically up and down, effectively both cutting and mashing the fish. Keep adding a few at a time and empty the contents frequently for ease. Using this method you can make enough chum for a day's sharking in a third of the time it take using the mincer.

It's a minor point, but if you do use a mincer, make sure you clean it fully at the first opportunity. If left, the blood and flesh will congeal, making your job far harder. Use only pilchard oil for lubricant and rust inhibitor. Manufactured oils taint the chum with alien scent. A quick modification of the exit plate on the mincer is well worth the effort. Drill some of the holes larger to allow the build-up of bone to pass through — it makes no difference to the consistency of the mix.

Mixing chum is messy. It gets over you, the decks, and the gunnels. Make sure before you commence to fish that all the decks are washed down and cleaned, preferably with a little detergent. This avoids the element of risk through slipping and, worse, of someone falling overboard. One last observation: if you come across commercial fishers hauling nets or gutting their catch, it may be worth taking advantage of the natural scent trail that follows the lifting of the nets, or the jettisoning of unwanted fish. So many dead and dying fish end up floating free that porbeagles are often in the vicinity. Bearing in mind to stay well clear of the boats involved, this is a useful thing to remember.

Now you can see how much work is involved in keeping the scent lane strong. Don't fall into the trap of 'it will do' — because it won't. Work hard on that scent trail, keep it powerful, and the porbeagles will come to you: it's far harder for you to find them.

CHAPTER 7

Bait Presentation

DEADBAIT

How the hook is positioned in the bait, and how the bait is presented when in the water, is very important. A hook point needs to be far enough away from the flesh of the fish to allow the point to find the shark's jaw as the line comes tight. If the point is masked by the baitfish's flesh, this can make the hook miss the target. On the other hand, should the hook point be too proud of the bait, the shark may feel the hard metal and instantly spit the bait out. This is one of the main reasons a good first run can end with the shark dropping the bait and failing to return. Sharks obviously have sensitive mouths and, as seen in Chapter 2, have some capacity to learn. They are accustomed to chomping straight through a baitfish, so it comes as no surprise that a shark spits the bait out when its jaws hit solid metal. When in position, the actual hook point should lie about 2cm (1in) proud of the flesh.

The problems we anglers have in presentation are caused by the additional weight we add through the hook-and-wire trace. A mackerel tossed overboard with no hook inside sinks slowly, twisting and turning as the tide dictates. The head tilts downwards in relation to the tail, but the rate of fall is slow. This gives us a basis to work from. There's little we can do about the fall rate without a great deal of work,

but at least we know that the bait should be presented head down. In addition, many porbeagles swim at a sharp, upward angle, and from beneath the bait, before simply scooping in the entire offering – as is the case with the smaller baits. A bigger bait will be taken from the side. After the first run, the shark will stop and turn the bait so that the head goes into the gullet first for ease of swallowing. It's clear from this that a hook needs to be positioned just to the rear of the head for the maximum opportunity of a hook up.

For static float fishing and deadbait free-lining, I take the baitfish (which ideally should be about 1 kg (2 lb) in weight or perhaps more) in my left hand, with the head touching my inside wrist. The hook's point is passed into the flesh just below the root of the tail. Feed this down and along the upper back (where the flesh is firm) until the gape of the hook allows no further travel. Note that the hook point travels inside the fish along the backbone. At no time does the hook pass through the opposite side. Bring the hook point out and pull a few centimetres of wire trace through the fish; re-insert the hook point a few centimetres further down and repeat. A third repetition of this process should see the hook positioned near the head. Leave the hook shank in the fish and gently draw any loose trace wire back into the fish until both leader and fish lie in a straight line. Take care not to tear the bait's skin when passing the hook through and pulling the trace tight. I also cut the tail fin off as this reduces the bait's tendency to spin as the tide catches the tail.

Some anglers prefer to tie the root of the tail to the wire trace for extra rigidity, but this is not really necessary. The best item for this is thin, elasticated cotton or shearing elastic. There is no need to knot this as it grips onto itself. This style of presentation really allows the shark to pulp the bait yet, on the whole, the bait will stay intact if the shark should drop it. This is also a useful technique in that the

leader follows the length of the backbone and is disguised.

Not a favourite method of mine, but nevertheless a fairly effective form of attachment, is putting the hook through the base of the tail where the meat starts to thicken. With the hook and a good length of trace pulled through, you take a complete turn around the baitfish's body. The hook is then passed through the gill cover to the inside of the mouth and the point comes out of the lower lip.

Although the hook point is well exposed and in the correct position for a

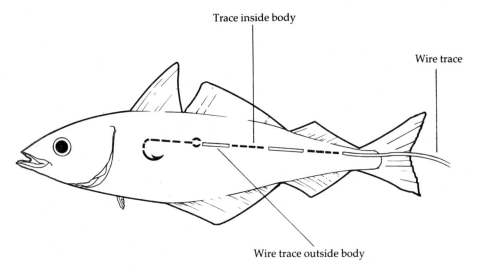

Trace inside body

Wire trace

Wire trace outside body

Figure 20: Threaded trace hook-mounting

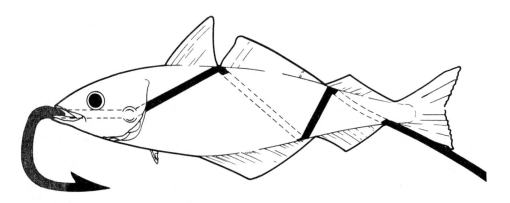

Figure 21: Wire-roll method of hook-mounting

good hook hold, should the shark drop the bait, the wire trace will (too often for my liking) tear free. This leaves the bait hanging head upwards held only by the hook. A further disadvantage is that the wire trace is fully exposed to the shark's teeth as its head is manoeuvred into the correct position for swallowing.

Bigger deadbaits – between 1 kg (2½ lb) and 2.5 kg (5 lb) need to be mounted on a double-hook rig. Hiding two hooks is obviously difficult. The method I prefer is to have two hooks on separate pieces of wire joined to a link loop (see Chapter 14). Pass the hook on the longest length of wire down the backbone as before. This needs to be positioned correctly with the leader taught before we set the second hook. This can be inserted down the flank or, better still, slit open a little of the belly to allow the whole hook to sit inside. Bring the point out of the body at a different angle to the first hook. The belly can either be roughly stitched shut or belly and body bound together with shearing elastic. The wire on the second hook need not be taut – the first hook (being in the stronger position) takes the bait's full weight.

When baitfish are in short supply, you may be unable to get single baits big enough to give a shark a good mouthful. It looks a little untidy and very unnatural, but you can get away with putting two small baits on the one hook. Don't consider placing two baits head to tail – this is too long and tends to spin underneath the float. I fish this rig by threading the one bait as before, just nicking the well-exposed point of the hook through the flank of the second bait, in the belly towards the back of the dorsal. As I say, this is not neat but does catch fish because of its bulk. This is something else to bear in mind: sharks may show little interest in one small bait but may be triggered into feeding by a big, bulky one – they tend to go for a greater mass.

I always slash the sides of my deadbaits to allow some emission of scent. The second bait on a two-bait rig benefits from having two deep cuts the full length of the backbone, made either side of the dorsal. This allows blood to spill but keeps the fish in a solid state. Make sure the secondary bait is the smaller one or porbeagles may be able to chop off the head below the hook.

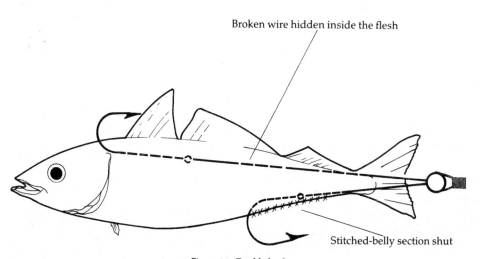

Broken wire hidden inside the flesh

Stitched-belly section shut

Figure 22: Double-hook rig

When sharks are cruising near the boat but refuse to hit a solid or free-lined deadbait, try a full, fresh fillet. Cut the fillet cleanly from the flank of a largish fresh fish, mount the thin end by pushing it up the hook shank and over the hook's eye onto the wire trace. This is then bound with shearing elastic. The wide end is brought through the hook twice and should lie straight. This disguises the hook a little yet gives a clean run for the point when the shark bites.

It's worth investigating floating and slow-sinking baits. We've already seen how slow-sinking fish locate the sharks' feeding zone. The question is, how do we slow down the rate of fall? I use small chunks of polystyrene. Cut the belly end of the baitfish open to allow the wire trace to be passed through from the mouth. The hook now sits inside the mouth with the point well clear. The polystyrene is then pushed into the gut cavity. The chunks should be about 1cm ($\frac{1}{2}$in) square. Five or six placed inside a bait weighing about $\frac{1}{2}$kg (1 lb) will ensure the rate of fall slows to a very gentle descent. This is all a balance between the weight of the hook (keeping the head downwards in a natural position) and the more buoyant tail partially supporting the whole structure.

The open belly section should be stitched together with a small baiting needle – but the curved needle used by leather workers is even better. Use either fine string or even monofilament in the 5 kg (12 lb) range at a pinch. Polystyrene is a good choice, being soft when the shark bites but breaking up easily.

Floating baits need much more buoyancy, as there is the added weight of the wire trace to consider. The best way is to incorporate a plastic bag, which needs to be fairly strong. This should be pushed down the deadbait's gullet, right into the gut cavity. The open end is, of course, left protruding from the fish's mouth. Partially inflate the bag, sealing the end with a half hitch. The knot is tucked into the back of the mouth. The hook must, it goes without saying, be in place before all this is attempted. The bag doesn't put the shark off as, when they bite, the bag doesn't pop like a burst balloon because it's enclosed in the baitfish. While mentioning balloons, it must be said that they are no good for this type of inflation. Anyone who has blown up a balloon will know they have a nasty rubbery taste. Don't take the chance – a porbeagle might be aware of the scent of rubber and leave the bait well alone.

Floating baits need to be used near the boat, otherwise seabirds will attack them. They are very effective on the calm days when sharks cruise around the boat just underneath the surface. To push the bag into place, I have made myself a special tool. You need a stainless-steel bar of 5mm ($\frac{1}{4}$in) in diameter and about 45cm (18in) long. This is then roughened at one end to form a handle. You can use either a small, drilled lead bullet or round piece of rubber glued to the end of the bar to push the bag into the gut cavity without damaging the bag. It's worth making a second such tool some 0.6m (2ft) in length for use on the larger fish.

I've tried squid as a deadbait but, as yet, have met with no success even though it's a popular bait in American waters. However, I have yet to try this when sharks are around the boat. The easiest method of mounting squid is on a single hook. This should be brought through the head between the eyes, the hook point facing away from the flowing tentacles. It's necessary to fix the squid's tail to the wire trace for good presentation. This is achieved by placing fine string over the wire just above where the squid's tail ends, and bringing the two pieces of string through the flesh about 1cm ($\frac{1}{2}$in) apart. These are gently knotted without tearing

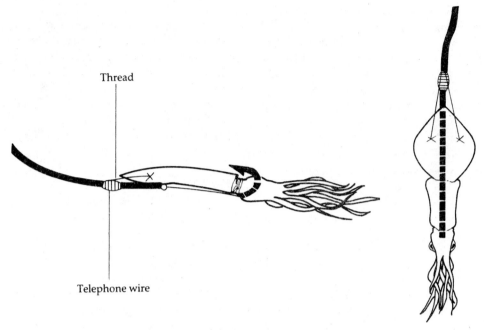

Thread

Telephone wire

Figure 23: Single hook-mounting for squid

the flesh and will hold the squid tight to the leader for normal fishing. To avoid the string sliding down the wire, I use a few turns of thin telephone wire just below the knot.

I'm currently trying a system that incorporates a wire flight. An eye is formed in the middle of a length of wire and bent upwards. The two legs are brought forward at an angle of 45 degrees and the ends bent over to form a barbless hook. These are hooked into the squid and hold the bait both steady and in a life-like fashion. Again, the addition of telephone wire stops the flight from sliding down the trace.

For those willing to put in extra effort, you can work a deadbait sink and draw. Choose a bait of at least 1 kg (2 lb) in weight. Slit the belly open and remove the stomach contents. With a sharp knife, sever the backbone just behind the head. This is done by working from inside the gut cavity. Remove the rest of the back-

bone either with the knife or by running your fingers along it. When you get to the tail section a further cut at the base of the backbone sees the whole skeleton come away. You are now left with a whole but very supple fish. The belly can now be sewn up. The hook is mounted simply by putting the point through both upper and lower lips. It's also prudent to cut off the tail fin to avoid spinning the bait on the retrieve.

In calm seas with little tide-run you can let the bait sink until it reaches a good depth, then slowly rewind, pausing occasionally to add a little more in the way of distress signals. A fast retrieve causes the bait's body to twist and bend with a most life-like swimming action. This also works in a good tide-run, although you need a little lead to keep the bait down when retrieving towards the boat. Bottom-fished deadbaits are made more attractive by filling the body cavity with the guts from other baitfish. This helps to create a strong scent trail to feed down-tide, hugging the seabed.

The addition of visual attractors is very much in its infancy, especially in the UK. Knowing that squid have those phosphorescent particles under their skin certainly suggests they would benefit from the addition of a cyalume light stick. Light sticks placed in baits fished at depth have caught fish. The reason for this is as yet not fully understood.

I don't favour the light source being placed on the wire trace just in front of the bait. I am always worried that a shark may go for the stick and miss the hook. Instead, I prefer to place the light stick inside the bait. First, I break the bait's backbone to give it some flexibility. I then slit the flanks of the fish wide open and enlarge the holes a little. The stick is placed inside, and I trust light will be emitted through the slashes in the flanks as the bait rolls with the tide. To me, this is more natural — a good simulation of plankton bursting into activity as baitfish move through. I feel a constant light source may be detrimental to a relatively static bait. The opposite, of course, would apply to a bait that continually moves.

An American angler (not directly involved in fishing for porbeagles) has experimented with baits dyed with con-fectionery colouring. With plenty of scope left for experimentation, he feels that colour makes little difference to the smaller predators he has concentrated on. I haven't tried this method but feel that the colouring will be invisible below 7m (25ft), and that any fish on the surface when viewed from below would be seen as black shapes. For my money, that's the end of the story.

LIVEBAIT

I have no hesitation in using livebait when shark-fishing — it's doubtful that porbeagles come across many dead fish in everyday life; everything is eaten alive. We must use this to our advantage whenever possible.

The offering of livebait to close-cruising sharks almost always sees them gain interest. You can suspend the livebait below the balloon as you would with a deadbait. This has the drawback of holding the bait at one level and relying on the shark coming to you. Free-lining is more effective. The bait sinks slowly and, while it struggles, it gives off those magic impulses that sharks find so irresistible. As the bait slowly sinks it searches out the feeding level where the sharks are swimming. When speed of presentation is needed, the

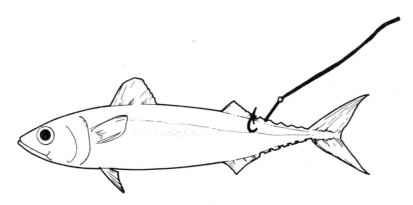

Figure 24: Hook through the tail of a livebait

hook can be passed cleanly through the tail, but avoid the lateral line and any vital organs.

The damage done to baitfish means they have only a short period of activity before they succumb to the loss of blood and the drag of the hook-and-wire trace. If the only livebait you have is small, then cut down on the size of hook you use when attaching through the tail. With the smaller mackerel, go down to an 8/0. The weight is less, its bulk is less, but hooking is good due to the well-exposed point. When you require a livebait to continue to swim for longer periods, it's important to avoid any physical damage that quickly weakens the fish. Also, if the livebait is not eaten by your quarry it can be returned alive to the water with the minimal amount of injury. Simply passing the hook point through the lower lip works. The bait swims quite well with only a small hole in the lower-lip membrane. It's a short-term solution, however, and doesn't allow the baitfish as much freedom as one would like.

For freedom we turn to a bridle rig. These are used extensively in America and elsewhere but rarely in the UK. I've used this system frequently and, providing you get the hook near to the snout of the baitfish, the number of successful hook-ups is high. Initially I was worried when experimenting with this rig as, by rights, it's a trolling rig used on big game; however, it has since proved excellent with free-lined baits. I leave the shark to eat the bait a fraction longer than normal. This does not increase the problems of gut-hooking — in fact, the opposite is the case. Most fish are hooked in the front jaw, either in the roof of the mouth or in the scissors.

The best bridle material is strong (but fine) string or cord. This knots well and is supple. More desirable is its lack of springiness — once knotted it stays knotted. Some anglers use 23 kg (50 lb) monofilament. However, in my opinion this is too springy and knots badly. Abrasion also worries me: mono easily scuffs when constantly moving against a metal hook shank. The fibre string does not.

I use a fine baiting needle. The length of string should be about 45cm (18in). Pass the needle through the top lip at a

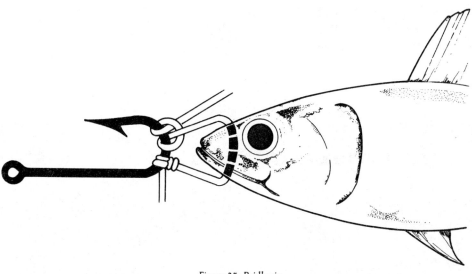

Figure 25: Bridle rig

point about 1cm ($\frac{1}{2}$in) behind the front edge of the lip. Increase this distance a little when using bigger baits. Keep the needle in a straight, vertical line and continue until the string in the needle's eye comes through into the mouth cavity. The needle continues its downward travel until the string comes through the membrane of the lower lip. You should now have a free end of string out of the upper lip and a free end of string from the lower lip.

Tie the end of the string coming from the lower lip to the hook shank with the knot shown in the diagram (p 63). Use the upper string to pull the hook into position. Trim the top piece of string to the required length and knot to the hook. If you prefer, use this system in exactly the same way, but only pass the string through the top lip. Aim to get the hook positioned about 1cm ($\frac{1}{2}$in) in front of the lips. Allow a little slack so that the mouth stays open, letting water over the gills.

This is an uncomplicated system and it is easy to master – even when at sea and conditions are bad. Although this connection is strong it does little harm to the bait and allows almost unrestricted swimming movement. I tend to stick with this rig, but some anglers prefer a bridle rig that, instead of running through the mouth, goes above the eyes and under-

neath the skull bone. I find this a too-cruel and unnecessary method. It keeps the fish alive for a long period and offers the hook in a slightly better position for the hooking of shark, but you can't return the livebait at the end of the session or when a new, more lively bait is required – and that is unacceptable.

In a similar way, the hook can be passed horizontally through the upper lips in front of the nostrils. This gives a firm anchorage providing you match the hook to the bait size. The fish will swim for a long period but, again, I find this unnecessary as it causes permanent damage.

It's not essential to learn all these different types of presentation; either a member of the crew or the skipper will happily do the job for you. On the other hand, you may wish to fish in areas where charter captains have only a basic knowledge and know little of modern thinking on sharking. Also, you may find it's far more enjoyable to hook a fish on a bait you've prepared yourself. The most important prerequisite for success is the ability to recognize the need to change tactics as the tide or weather conditions change throughout the day. It's the skipper's job to look after you and the boat and ultimately locate the sharks. The job of actually catching them is yours.

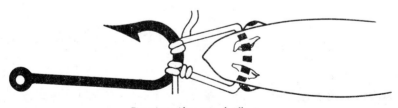

Figure 26: Alternative bridle rig

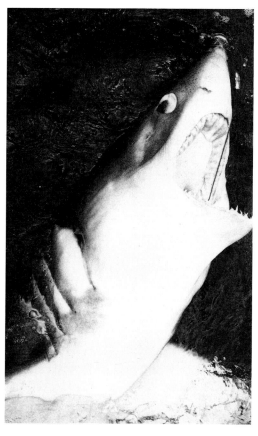

A 68-kg (150-lb) fish rolls on its back before diving away from the boat

This 57-kg (125-lb) fish is about to try to bite a chunk out of the boat

This porbeagle thrashes the water to foam as it's held on the trace

As it passes the boat, this porbeagle starts to spin. Look closely — the dorsal fin is in the water and the pectoral stands erect

A 68-kg (150-lb) fish swims past the boat to have a look at the occupants

This photograph illustrates the streamlined shape of the porbeagle

The jaws

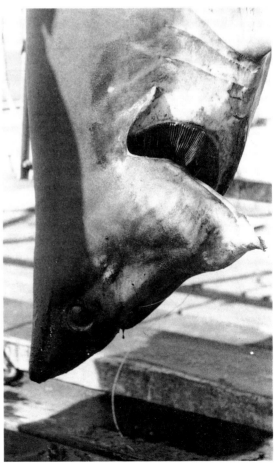

Shot of the gill composition

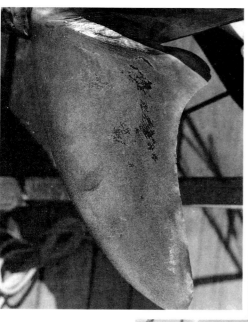

The dorsal fin. Note the white mark at the base

A porbeagle's tail fin

The shape of a porbeagle's pectoral fin

A small pup being released

The ampullae of Lorenzini are clearly marked on the nose of this porbeagle. These sensors are believed to pick up electrical impulses in the search for prey

A unique photograph. On the right, John Mears of Derby, England, the previous Welsh record-holder, and the author (dark shirt) with that 93-kg (205-lb) fish

Shark-fishing is often a waiting game

It's important to keep full pressure on the shark at all times

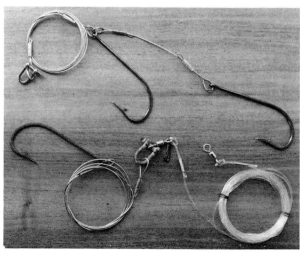

Top: a two-hook rig for big baits. Bottom: single-hook rig and mono leader. Note in both cases the U-shackle link for strength

Cutting a 68-kg (150-lb) shark free at the side of the boat

Porbeagles often become foul-hooked during their initial attack. The hook can be clearly seen outside the mouth

It was a stroke of good fortune that photographer
Russell Symons happened to be on board the Lady
Jayne when Brian Taylor hooked a world-record
porgie off Padstow in Cornwall. In the picture above
he plays the shark at the beginning of the struggle on
8-kg tackle.

(ABOVE RIGHT) The shark attempts to cut the line by
diving under the boat

(RIGHT) The shark had to be craned inboard. It was
obviously a record for 16-lb line

(OPPOSITE) Back to port with the 382-lb monster; a
world record in the 8-kg (16-lb) class

This illustrates how careful you must be to avoid getting your hands and arms tangled in the wire trace

This shark has spun, wrapping the trace several times around the body. This needs to be freed before the hook is removed

This 57-kg (125-lb) fish is about
to be freed. The wire should be cut
as close to the mouth as possible.
The remaining hook will soon rot
or fall out

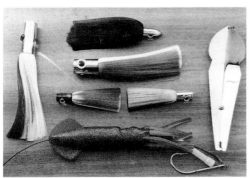

A selection of the trolling lures, an imitation squid, and
metal spoon used by the author

The barrel and link used to retain big shark when
fishing from small boats. Also included is a standard
wire tailer and two, metal, hook disgorgers easily
made at home

An 88-kg (194-lb) porbeagle taken from Cardigan Bay in Wales

The jaws of a 90-kg (200-lb) porbeagle in relation to a man's leg

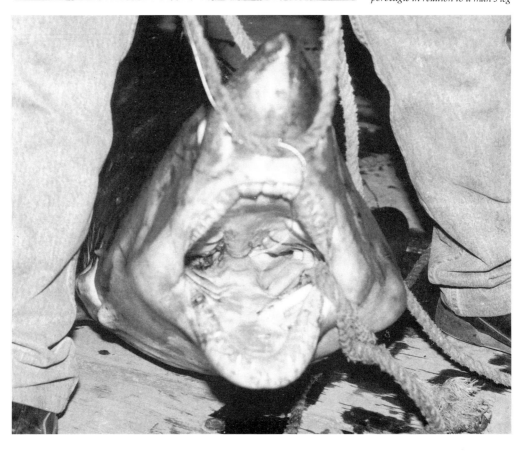

Top: a Sampo ball-bearing snap link. Left to right: a Berkley swivel; a Mustad rolling swivel size 5/0; a Dexter ball-bearing swivel; a Dexter heavy-duty game-fishing swivel. (All these are quality products and very strong for a given size. The last swivel is a cheap oriental barrel swivel and should be avoided.)

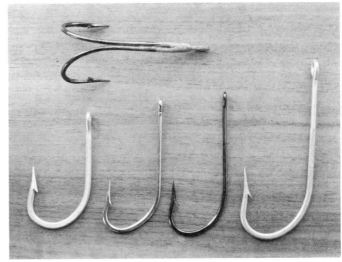

Top: a home-made double hook for trolling. Left to right: the superb Mustad Sea Demon size 12/0; a Diamond Yamamoto size 12/0; a 12/0 Mustad Bronzed O'Shaugnessy; a 14/0 Mustad long shank

Working clockwise; a light-weight Daiwa lever drag for light-line fishing; a Penn 6/0 for 30-class work; a Penn 9/0 for 50-class line; the Abu 10,000c for 20-class use

Lifting a small porbeagle into the boat for hook removal

Note the wonderfully streamlined shape of the porbeagle head

CHAPTER 8

Fishing at Anchor

Shark anglers everywhere rehearse the arguments for and against fishing on the drift and fishing at anchor. Drift fishing means that you cover a large area and your baits are given some natural movement by the tide. However, the arguments for drift fishing begin to lose credence when you consider that the chum trail is far less effective than when at anchor: with the boat at anchor (bow-on to the tide) the slick travels with the tidal current and covers a greater distance. This tends to locate sharks and bring them to you.

The area covered on the drift does not necessarily find fish.

A good captain uses anchorage to position the boat in such a way as to maximize the chum trail's advantage, over ground the captain either knows or feels is likely to hold shark. In those rocky reefs we've been discussing, you can either use the tide to take the chum over the actual reef and through all the nooks, crannies, and overhangs, or let the slick travel with the ever-present tidal currents at the reef's end to locate the shark that may well be lying

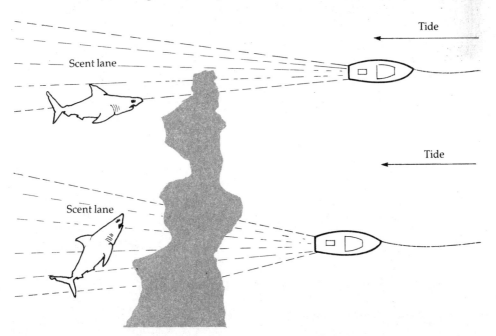

Figure 27: Correct anchoring to maximize the effects of chum

well downtide. When a particular shelf or bank is to be fished, the boat is anchored uptide of the mark. The anchor line is slowly paid out so that, when the boat is in position, baits released from the stern will actually fish on the drop-off.

Boats anchored above the heads of gutters take advantage of some tide movement to spread the chum trail. Alternatively, you can position the boat at the edge of a small tidal eddy that will hold balloon-suspended baits and concentrate the rubby-dubby. The major disadvantage of anchoring is the problem of the anchor rope. Many sharks head straight for the rope, wrapping the line around it several times during the fight. The policy of many modern shark boats is either to buoy the anchor off (retrieving this later) or, better still, to haul the anchor back into the boat if time allows. The problem with hauling the anchor is that the chum trail is broken. This severely disrupts prospects for the rest of the day and time is wasted re-establishing the scent lane when the boat returns to the same spot. There's a fine distinction between staying put when fighting a shark or releasing and drifting. I prefer to leave the anchor in place and assess the situation as it develops, so that the size of shark being fought can be gauged.

PREPARATION

When the boat steadies, the first step is to begin catching a few baitfish. I find it best if one or two anglers take on this important task, which also puts some distress signals into the water. Much depends on the steaming time it has taken to reach the grounds and whether or not your tackle is ready. I'm not happy threading line, tying knots, etc., when the boat is in motion. Fish can be lost this way through a lack of care. There's also a safety factor involved: a large shark hook could be buried in someone should they fall with the boat's motion.

If a maximum of four anglers are to fish, two should start on the bait while the other two make ready their tackle. The skipper usually sees to the dubby,

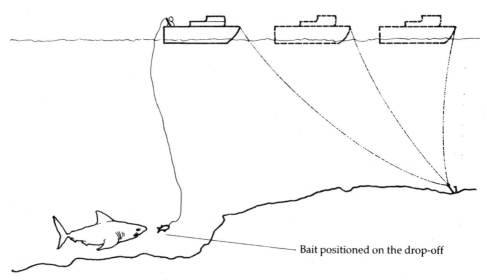

Bait positioned on the drop-off

Figure 28: Boat is released backwards on the anchor rope until baitfish is on the drop-off

although the anglers should be prepared to accept the responsibility for this themselves. The chum bags need to be in the water at the earliest opportunity. An agreement as to the distance each angler will fish from the boat should be decided democratically, either by the skipper or by the anglers drawing straws, etc.

In Chapter 6 on chum, we saw how the angle of scent deepens the further away from the boat it goes. We have to consider this, as well as the speed of the passing tide, when we set the depth of the balloon floats. In water of a moderate depth, say 30m (100ft), I prefer to have the furthest balloon at a depth of 12m (35ft). This is measured in the following manner. Roughly work out the length of your wire trace and leader, and then count the length of needed line by spanning the distance between the middle of your chest and an outstretched arm, until the target is reached. When the required depth of line is attained, lock the balloon into position.

An elastic band is best for this as it doesn't damage the line and is soft enough to pass through the rod rings when a shark is being fought to the side of the boat. Select only those rubber bands that are 1cm ($\frac{1}{2}$in) wide with a length of about 8cm (3in). Place the band horizontally underneath the line, bring one of the loops over the line and through the centre of the other loop and tighten. This locks the band in place and will not move if done properly.

The party balloon should be inflated to the size of an average grapefruit (slightly larger for bigger baits). The tail of the balloon is held firmly shut and passed through the open loop of the rubber band. Now knot the balloon's tail over the rubber band with a couple of half-hitches. If you prefer, use a small free-running swivel: a short length of mono no more than 3–5kg (8 lb) breaking strain connects the swivel to the balloon. The swivel butts up to the rubber band for depth position. Some anglers use a short piece of PVC tubing and a match. When the correct depth has been ascertained, form a loop in the line. The head of the loop goes over the base of the match stalk and is pushed up inside the tube. When a shark pulls the line tight, the line pulls free from the tube. I dislike this method – the line could be damaged with resulting weakness.

When all is ready, don't just drop the baited trace straight over the side: with any amount of tide-run your bait will lift with the water pressure and be on the surface. Allow for enough weight of lead to keep the bait down during the strongest tide-run you expect that day. The last thing you want is to have to keep recovering your bait and adding more lead. I put a small torpedo link onto the upper hook-trace loop and attach a streamlined lead of around 170gm (6 oz) or use spiral leads wound onto the upper leader. If you require the lead to fall away on the strike, use weak mono that will break.

Lower the bait gently over the side paying out the leader and line to avoid tangles. Check the blloon sits correctly, being neither too buoyant through over-inflation and hence causing excessive drag to a taking shark, nor almost submerged. It's prudent to have the reel in free spool with the check on – just in case a run should develop straight away (this happens). Pay out some 70m (80yd) of line; the ratchet is now disengaged, and light pressure from your thumb avoids any tendency for the reel to over-run. Re-engage the ratchet but leave the reel in free spool when the balloon reaches the correct position.

In a fast tide, the ratchet on its own may not offer enough resistance to stop the tide taking line from the spool due to the pressure on the line and bait. If this happens, attach another rubber band with a half-hitch to the line just above the reel.

Either put the free end of the loop over the harness lugs or on the screws that hold the reel clamp. This will simply break and fly off when a shark runs, but will stop the line from being dragged from the spool by the tide.

When tides are slack, the reel line between rod tip and balloon will sink in the water. To aid striking and to prevent a free-swimming shark getting tangled, put a slit in three bottle corks and slide these on your line at intervals as you pay out line. These fall off when a shark takes. The rod should be left slightly inclined up by the stern, either tied or (preferably) clipped to a cleat or some other solid structure that is part of the boat. I use a 1-m (1-yd) length of 10-mm ($\frac{1}{2}$-in) climbing rope with a large, split-link climbing karabiner. This either fastens round the rod or clips to one of the reel bars. Rods go over the side, so take good care. Finally, check and double check that the line can leave the reel freely with the ratchet engaged.

The angler designated the second balloon should deliberately choose a different colour of balloon for ease of identification, should a run occur. The depth of the second bait should be set at 10m (30ft) and positioned 55m (60yd) off the stern. These two anglers now take over bait-catching duties.

The third set of tackle sits 7m (25ft) deep and 35m (40yds) out. For the fourth set of tackle you have a choice: either set it up as float gear, say 4–6m (12–18ft) deep and 18m (20yd) out, or simply drop it over the side with just enough lead to hold it in the tide. The latter system pays dividends – you avoid the dense pattern that can cause tangles yet it plays on the porbeagle's habit of sitting underneath the boat casually surveying the scene. This pattern of depth is aimed at the shark that picks the scent trail up while bottom swimming, responding to the strengthening smell by lifting in the water. Likewise, we have a bait at a likely depth for a shark that comes in at a set level of depth.

Some anglers feel at a disadvantage when placed close to the boat but, in practice, you have no reduced chances. There may be an argument that, on clear,

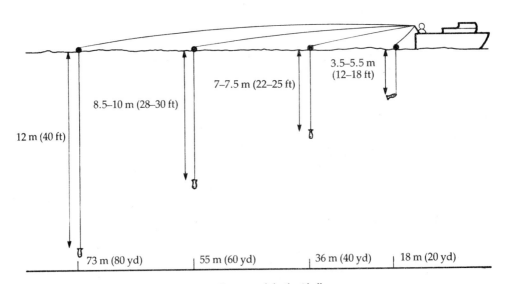

Figure 29: Pattern and depth of balloons

still days when the water clarity is high, the furthest balloons seem to do the best. Add a little cloud cover or a short chop to the surface water, and the inside balloons are often the first to go.

Weird things can happen to balloons when the tide is slack and a breeze dictates a boat's position: balloons refuse to leave the side of the boat when in the water; they head up past the bow and sit over the anchor rope; worse still, as the boat swings on the anchor, they shift from the starboard to port bow and back again. Lines can chafe on the hull or superstructure and should be checked for abrasion. This is the worst time for a shark to take a bait. There's little you can do about these problems except to wait for the tide to turn. The increase in flow will adjust the position of the baloons.

The slick can be seen easily on rougher days by the line of calmer water created by the oil from the fish rising to the surface. However, this may be a surface drift caused by wind. The balloons may be 18m (20yd) away from this, yet actually be sitting right in the middle of the scent avenue. This occurs when a slight side wind pushes the surface slick off at an angle but hasn't the power to over-rule the tide and so shift the balloon.

If any weed should foul one of the lines this must be retrieved immediately to avoid tangling other lines. Often, the balloons are offset to each other in a staggered pattern and retrieval is easy. Even when they lie in a straight line a little deft manoeuvring can bring them back so that they can be paid out again without tangling the other lines. When doing this, watch for a shark grabbing the moving bait: again, a bad time for this to happen for they knit all the lines together – something that unfortunately occurs frequently.

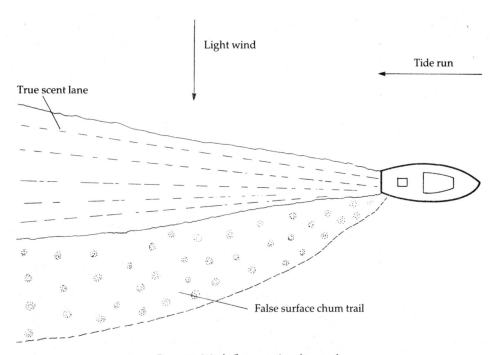

Figure 30: Wind effect on surface chum trail

FIRST RUN

Invariably, you never see the shark that takes the first bait. Some takes can come as the first balloon is being fed away from the boat. Usually it takes the chum a couple of hours to find them. Most anglers let their eyes wander from the float, either by talking to others or by eating, catching bait, and even dozing off. We all do it, but I try to be observant, watching and learning the pattern of the balloon as it rises and falls in the swell. In doing this, and in realizing that the pattern of movement has been broken, I often have my rod clipped free from its safety cord held ready in my hand before the shark starts its first run. This is a big advantage; I believe that even the drag of the ratchet can spook some fish into dropping the bait. The balloon may lift out of the water and lie flat as the shark takes the bait while swimming upwards at an almost vertical angle. Three or four distinct bobs of the balloon followed by its sudden disappearance is a characteristic take. Sometimes the balloon darts sideways or simply vanishes in an instant. Other sharks bounce the balloon four or five times in a series of attempts before final acceptance. Underwater, the balloon bursts because of water pressure. It is impossible to categorize the bites porbeagles may give — simply expect the unexpected.

I always unclick the ratchet, using the ball of my thumb to smooth the coils of line from lifting as the shark begins to run. In this way you become tuned into the behaviour of your fish. This pre-acceptance run takes between 27 and 64m (30 and 70yd) of line. When the line stops running from the spool there is a pause, which lasts for only a couple of seconds before you feel three or four gentle knocks. This is the shark turning and swallowing the bait. When these stop it's your cue to re-engage the spool lever and wait.

The drag on the clutch has been pre-set to give line under a moderate pressure. As the shark swims away, simply let the line tighten into the weight of the fish that, providing your hook is sharp, easily sinks the hook past the barb. Forget striking the fish by lifting the rod tip vertical — the bow in the line produces minimum hook pressure at any distance, and you've the weight of the lead and wire trace to move before you pressurize the hook. It is this steady pressure from the tight line that pulls the hook home.

Don't expect the shark to make a mad dash for freedom at this stage. This may happen — but not always. Little fish are usually the ones to bolt. Most fish move sideways or at an angle to the tide. When you realize the direction the shark has decided on, the anglers responsible for any balloons inside the taken bait should retrieve them as quickly as possible. Balloons beyond the hooked shark must be brought in to the boat when the shark is out at one side of the stern. This sounds risky (and it is), but surprisingly few tangles occur. When lines do become crossed they are in a terrible mess. Vigilance, common sense, and calm, rational thought save the situation.

Some large fish seem to follow a pattern of swimming uptide some way before veering off and running at an angle to the tide. Very fast runs from large fish are rare; their runs are methodical and conducted at a moderate pace, but they do go on and on. Small pups strip some 27–55m (30–60yd) of line rapidly before quietening down. Generally, sharks keep running with short, in-between pauses, when they sulk or hug the bottom. These runs are rarely more than 45m (50yd), although the odd male fish in the 45–68-kg (100–150-lb) group may really hammer off, taking well over 100m of line before slowing. Some sharks like to fight it out on the surface, with plenty of tail splashing.

These are the ones that literally spin their bodies in the water until the weak reel line finds tough skin and the connection parts.

Large and small fish may occasionally breech surface water in a porpoise-type roll. I have personally never seen a porbeagle leap in mako fashion, but some skippers tell me this happens. This can cause problems if the shark goes away from the boat and breaks water — as already said, this is a sure sign they are going to roll. Make sure there is no slack line between the rod tip and the fish to decrease the chance of fish and line coming into contact.

Big fish frequently run out more than 275m (300yd) of line, then instantly double back — often coming in deep, right underneath the boat. This is a dangerous time. Shark reels are relatively slow on the retrieve, and it takes time to re-gain that lost line. If the hook is not in solid jaw-tissue, it may fall out as the line comes slack. Equally likely is that the shark may rest for a few moments then move off. In this situation, when a shark comes back towards me, I ease the clutch pressure and watch where the line enters the water while reeling in. Watching the line gives prior warning of a shark's fresh change in direction; it tells you to stop reeling and that the light clutch will give line easily when the line comes tight. Leaving the clutch on a hard setting is to court disaster. If the shark hits full speed after a sulking period, and the angler is unaware of this and is still retrieving line, the pressure on the line (as it comes tight) rises from nothing in a single second to the full water weight of the shark. This simply overloads the line, which parts — usually within a few centimetres of the reel.

Sometimes the fish sit on the bottom and refuse to move, except in small circles. It's harder for the angler to maintain an upward pressure with the rod than it is for the shark to keep a downward pull on the line. However, steady pressure from the rod ensures the shark eventually gives in.

Shark that let themselves be easily led back to the boat after a couple of good runs are being crafty. They will come inward and upward towards the stern, often appearing suddenly on the surface. A quick burst of power surges through their bodies to the tail. They change direction and veer right or left and run. These runs are often the longest, exceeding 90m (100yd). Another disconcerting habit of a shark that comes back to the boat is when it appears on the surface, just to the rear of the stern. It slowly swims with both fin and head out of the water along the length of the boat's hull. This shark is likely to be less than 2m (6ft) from the angler; you look right into its eyes and it into yours. Anglers who've experienced this say it's a bloodcurdling confrontation. I believe this is deliberate: they want to see what is the cause of their dilemma. I've noticed that, when these shark have passed the cockpit where the crew are standing, they sound.

I've known very large fish take 360m (400yd) of line on the first run. These fish are slow but totally unstoppable. Never let the capacity of the reel fall below 180m (200yd) without telling the skipper. It is also prudent to have the engines on tick-over so that the fish can be followed if need be. Such fish tend to mastermind the whole battle at a distance. This is helpful, for not only will the rod exert pressure on the shark but also the amount of line between the angler and the fish is subjected to pressure by the weight of water it displaces — gradually sapping the shark's strength.

Sharks of all sizes will shake their heads from side to side and try to rub the hook out on the seabed. Many caught sharks have scuff marks along their underjaw and belly where they've touched the seabed. A favourite trick is for them to circle the boat slowly so that the rod has to be passed under the anchor rope, which is unsafe in a lumpy sea. I've seen shark circumnavigate the boat half a dozen times. These fish are the most likely to make a sudden dash underneath the boat where the line may touch the hull and part. A fighting shark may respond to the engines – it is a fact that they will increase speed as the engine's revs rise. I prefer to have the engines quiet at all times except when line capacity is critical.

An interesting point that I'm sure is associated to basic intelligence, is the shark's purposeful direction. Porbeagles, usually the larger specimens, may appear at first to fight in an unorthodox style yet careful observation will show they are persistently returning to the same heading. For instance, I once fought a porbeagle for five hours. This female made a persistent effort to reach a large buoy that marked the edge of a shallow, rocky reef. She towed an 8-m (27-ft) boat close on 4 miles (6.5km) from the original hook-up point before she was secured. Her choice of direction was sideways onto a steady tide-run. Sharks seem to know that the chance of reaching a static feature offers the hope of release. This could be (and probably is) the reason they head for the anchor rope or dart under the hull.

Some sharks can be subdued in minutes, irrespective of their size. Others – not necessarily the biggest – can take hours: it's all a matter of attitude and, to a lesser extent, the barometric pressure prevalent at the time. Sharks have characters similar to humans. Some are mentally weak and give up before the battle commences. Others fight for a short period then throw in the towel. A number are stubborn, aggressive, clever, and flatly refuse to give up. These shark may weigh as little as 68 kg (150 lb), yet can take two or three hours to beat on lightish tackle. A shark in excess of 136 kg (300 lb) with this type

of character is a tremendous opponent. They will push even very experienced anglers who have much larger fish to their credit to the very limit of their physical and mental capabilities.

At times of very high barometric pressure, sharks become lethargic. They do not feed well at this time. However, any fish that are hooked are picky, disturbing the balloon many times before taking it under. When hooked they won't run, they just stay on the surface, rolling over belly up. I've experienced 45-kg (100-lb) fish brought straight to the boat and released in under four minutes without scarcely any attempt at an escape. It's usually during these periods of high barometric pressure that sharks will either pull the float under and then release the bait or run a short distance and drop it. The astute angler does not wait in the hope that the shark will return, even though it may. Instead, gently and very slowly start to reel the line in. The bait starts to move in the water. Keep the slow retrieve going until you bring the bait back to the stern of the boat. The shark probably sees the bait as a wounded fish attempting a feeble escape. This is enough to trigger an attack. You will be amazed at how gently the bait is taken under these circumstances. With the necessary slow retrieve the bait just stops, refusing to travel forward. You feel the shark (which may be only 6m (20ft) away from you) adjust the bait in its mouth, slowly turn, and then swim away. The angler is in a remarkable position at such times – at one with the fish, the rod offering a unique link with the power and thought of a wild creature.

Most sharks are lost in the latter stages of the fight, not by the hook falling out but by lack of thought on the angler's part about manipulation of tackle and mistakes both by the other anglers and, all too frequently, by an inexperienced skipper. Good skippers make it look easy; bad ones

72

lose you the fish. The angler is responsible for leading the shark to the boat. Only an experienced shark angler and skipper will know when a fish is beaten and tired. It may float side or belly up for a few seconds before rolling upright. It may swim in tight circles with no real purpose or may just hang in the tide.

The angler helps the crew by walking to the opposite side of the boat to bring the leader within reach of the crew. As soon as the leader is held by someone, the angler reduces drag on the reel to nil. If the shark should gain strength and bolt, the angler need only apply a little pressure with the ball of the thumb to avoid an over-run of line. The shark can take line from the spool without any undue pressure being placed on the line, which would otherwise break.

Whoever holds the wire trace should do so wearing strong, industrial gloves, using only enough force to hold the weight of the shark's head in the water. Never wrap the trace around your hand. If the shark should decide to dive, the wire will sever your fingers like a cheese cutter. A pair of long-nosed bolt-cutters is used to cut the wire trace as close to the mouth as possible. The hook left in the shark will rot away quickly and does no harm.

Shark to be returned alive should not be lifted into the boat, the only exception being young pups lightly hooked that would benefit from the hook being removed. These are light enough to be lifted with the body supported so that no internal damage results to the vital organs. This is obviously not possible with fish much over 20 kg (50 lb). Lay the pup on the deck, belly down. Kneel on the floor sitting gently over the fish. A second person steadying the tail by wedging it gently against a solid structure also helps. The person kneeling over the shark gently lifts the upper jaw by pulling back on the snout to allow access to the mouth for a

third person to remove the hook. This sounds fraught with danger but is less frightening in reality and does avoid undue stress to the shark.

A fish to be brought in for weighing needs to be kept in good condition to maintain its weight. I completely disagree with gaffing sharks. This is barbaric and leads to a massive loss of blood. Some ill-informed people suggest the best place to gaff a shark is in its belly, which is appalling and totally unproductive. The sheer weight of the fish can tear the flesh, releasing the shark with horrific wounds and still with almost full manoeuvrability. Live sharks with loose gaffs flying about should never be brought onto a boat. The only occasions I would consider a gaff are to secure a very large shark – and then only using it to steady the fish while it was being properly tailed and made fast to an aft cleat – or from the shore. If you absolutely must gaff a shark, do so in the underside of the lower jaw where only flesh will be damaged.

TAILING

Tailing shark is the best method and it is relatively easy once you've got the hang of it. It is also the quickest and most effective means of disabling a shark. Once its tail is out of the water, the fish has lost most of its power and all of its propulsion. There are two ways to tail. A rope about 7m (25ft) long and at least 2cm (1in) in diameter is formed into a loop with a free-sliding knot to allow the noose to close. The loop is laid open on the floor and the angler steps inside. A member of the crew stands level with the shark's tail, lifting the noose over the angler, up and over the rod and down the line. The noose is then fed over the shark, being drawn tight at the tail. This needs to be done in the minimum amount of time. I've used this system but I am not happy recommending it: you rely too heavily on the fish remaining still. There is also the boat's movement to be taken into consideration, which can disrupt the flow of the noose around the angler and along the shark. The dorsal fin is not easily negotiated. Instead, I prefer either a rope or purpose-made wire tailer that is applied directly over the tail. A heavy rope of a good diameter will hold the shape of the noose when submerged, although heavy wire is better. Rope is my first choice as this does less damage to the fish; wire can actually cut through the flesh if it's too thin.

When the tailer is in place around the shark's tail, the shark should be pulled half out of the water with the rope and then secured to a stout stern cleat. Held in this way, sharks may remain alive for a couple of hours, so leave plenty of time to elapse before handling them. If a big shark needs to be killed quickly, attach a second strong rope to the tail. The ropes go to separate cleats but must be of equal lengths and should be long enough to keep the shark's head at water level. Start the motors and tow the shark slowly behind the boat for thirty minutes. The reversal of water through its gills will effectively drown it.

Never try to club the shark across its head. This does little good, only serving to disturb the shark more and increase its futile efforts to escape. I've heard of people missing the shark and damaging decking and, worse, the outside of the hull. Never try to retrieve a hook from a supposedly dead shark until five or six hours have elapsed since capture. Even then, do it carefully just to be safe.

As soon as a hooked shark is landed, the other tackle should be put out again, for several shark tend to come in short periods with gaps of inactivity in between. The lucky angler should now take an inside position to allow the other members of the party full fishing time.

CONSERVING ENERGY

More experienced anglers have learned to pace themselves during a fight with a shark. If you know the fish is small, you can quickly pile the pressure on and boat the shark quickly. An unseen adversary could be any size and needs careful evaluation. The most effective angle for the rod to put maximum pressure on the fish is roughly 45 degrees. The angler needs to keep the rod bent to a minimum of a quarter circle and a maximum of a third of a circle. A butt pad to protect the groin is not essential, but it does add protection and acts as a pivot for the rod butt to centre on. In Britain (unlike the US) few if any boats have the facility of a fighting chair. With fish up to about 225 kg (500 lb) there is little real need for them. The angler must stand for the full duration and, at the same time, keep relentless rod pressure on the fish as well as reacting to the boat's movement in a lively sea. This obviously saps energy rapidly.

The most economic stance for the conservation of energy is when the angler's feet are aimed at the clock-face position of one fifty-five and about 2ft apart. The knees should be slightly bent. This gives the angler a point of balance against the shark. The fish's weight bends the rod, which imparts forward pull on the angler. If the angler adopts the above stance, knees slightly bent push the angler's weight backwards. This increases pressure on the shark with minimal loss of energy to the angler. The upper body should remain upright to avoid strain on the lower back muscles, as these are the first to hurt during a prolonged fight. The left arm should (for a right-handed person) be almost straight out in front of you, with the elbow slightly bent. The left hand grips the rod on the upperhand-grip (the upper forearm muscles are next to complain).

I try to rest when the shark is hanging in the tide, refusing to move of its own accord or by the pumping of the rod. I swap hands – but don't hold the rod on the upperhand-grip with your right hand. Place it instead just above the hand-grip. This allows a speedy swap for the left hand straight onto the grip when the fish begins to move.

After about two hours the shoulder and neck muscles start to ache. This is mainly caused by the unconscious effort of keeping your head downward looking at the reel as you give and take line. Minimize this by making a point of watching the line as it enters the water, or look to the horizon except when re-gaining line.

The worst experience for any angler is the approach of total fatigue. This is an unlikely part of porbeagle fishing, but two fish have pushed me close to the limits and other anglers, who have hooked bigger-than-average fish, have come close and many have succumbed. Being fit and relatively strong helps your stamina, but does not assure absolute immunity. The first sign is losing the feeling in your arms and your upper thighs getting spasms of a tingling sensation. Your knees submit and begin to shake uncontrollably – a muscle inflection. Close to the point of no return, the whole body begins to shake and lose all co-ordination. It's about now that many people feel the fish is not worth it; they drop the rod tip and some even beg for the line to be cut. A good skipper will rightly take offence at this act of submission, as will a real angler. It's an act almost akin to combat cowardice to cut a fish free.

Your biggest expenditure of effort is made when pumping the shark nearer to the boat in order to re-gain line. Trying to pull the rod tip back a metre or so each time against a reluctant fish soon tires you. It's easier if you use short, frequent pumps of the rod, say 15cm (6in). Lift the rod to an almost vertical position, simultaneously drop the rod tip, and reel the slack line in – then repeat. You can feel the shark add more resistance as you reach the upper end of the lift. They respond to being involuntarily led. Never lift the rod to the full vertical position – you lose control as you reach full height and this also creates too much slack line.

When a shark is heavy and hanging in the tide and you swap hands, you must still keep the rod fully bent in that third circle. If the shark stalls and refuses to take line, it is resting. Don't allow that rest to happen – you can often re-gain a metre or so of line before the pressure makes the shark move off once more.

On hot days, mild dehydration can be a problem. The occasional drink helps. Wear a hat to avoid the worst of the sun's rays. Most anglers prefer a baseball-type cap with a peak, but they tend to make you perspire. Sweat, which you lose in copious quantities on a hot day, can be a nightmare. It runs into your eyes and almost blinds you until you can't see to lay the line on the spool. I go prepared with either a towelling head-band or wrist-bands as worn by tennis players. You can wear a leather or PVC harness that clips onto the available lugs on the reel. This helps to take the pressure off the body for a while, but it creates a lazy angler with correspondingly longer fights. You come to rely on the harness to ease some of the burden, with less effective pressure from the rod directed at the shark.

As a final comment on the strain a fish can exert on you (and itself), consider a shark that fights strongly until it makes a last all-out crash-dive for the seabed. You can actually feel the fish smash into the bottom. When it does this you know the fish is dead. It will have put everything into the dive – its heart has simply given out. This has happened to me and to others; I sincerely hope it never happens to my readers. The task that follows can only be described as sheer agony. You must lift the full weight of the shark by the rod alone. The buoyant effect of the water helps, and lines over 13 kg (30 lb) are strong enough to lift most fish (providing the line is good quality), but it hurts the angler. The rod works as a lever against you. The dead weight of the fish must be pumped up bit by bit. With a large fish, this means short pumps and only centimetres of line retrieved at a time. This puts unbelievable strain on the back and leg muscles, leaving you stiff and sore for days.

The knack to lifting a dead fish is not to lift the rod too high, and no more than just above head height. When you drop the rod tip to re-gain line, do so in a controlled manner. If the rod tip is dropped too quickly the fish begins to sink and too much slack line is created by the rapidly dropping rod tip. Because the angler is already retrieving line, as it comes tight against the falling fish it is put under great strain and will break. You must keep the reel drag set well below the breaking strain of the line but, at the same time, you can't afford to give line. I keep the feel of the fish on the line as I drop the rod tip, adding gentle thumb pressure to hold the fish before the next up-sweep. This is a delicate business, and luck plays a great part in the landing of a dead fish.

A system I've tried with success in the past is a technique that uses the boat to lift the fish. The idea is to motor away from the dead shark very slowly, with the angler releasing line. A distance of about 90m (100yd) or more is needed, although this needs to be more in deeper water. The angler begins to pump the shark up as normal, but you must keep the pumps of the rod going continuously. You will feel the fish as a dead weight to begin with, but as its starts to move things become easier. The dead shark slowly lifts from

the bottom because of the shallower angle of the line. If you stop working the fish it will sink and all the hard work has been for nothing.

Using this technique you can get the shark within a metre or so of the stern so that one of the crew or one of your companions can grab the strong leader. This is by no means a foolproof system, but with hard work and common sense from the angler (and a little deft throttle control on the part of the skipper), it gives you a better return of 'landed fish' than a direct lift off the seabed. This technique is safer with 20–35-kg (50–80-lb) class tackle, but you will need a gentle touch when using 13.5-kg (30-lb) tackle. Lifting fish on lines below 13.5-kg (30-lb) class is almost impossible if the fish is of any size.

LEDGERING

Float-fishing or free-lining is not the only effective way of taking sharks. In early spring, sharks will hunt for much of their food on the seabed. This is obviously the time to ledger big baits. Ledgering for porbeagles rarely gets a mention, mainly because too many anglers and skippers are set in their ways. Shark tackle stays basically the same, but I prefer to change my customary 112-kg (250-lb) monofilament leader for an all-wire trace 5m (15ft) long. This protects the trace from major damage while on the seabed.

I never use really light line for ledger fishing (even over clean sand) preferring at least 10-kg (20-lb) tackle. I use a small, free-running swivel on the main line to which I attach a short length of mono and a lead heavy enough to keep the bait down. The short length of mono should be about 3-kg (6-lb) breaking strain so that, when the shark begins to fight, the lead will break free.

Often in the deeper water where less

tide-run is evident, the weight of the bait alone will be enough to take the tackle to the bottom. I like to use big baits for ledgering. Baitfish of at least 1kg (2 lb) – and preferably bigger – are needed to keep dogfish, tope, and other predators at bay.

Porbeagles give a simple indication of interest in a ledgered bait. I constantly watch the rod tip, for this will knock two or three times before any line is pulled from the spool. The knocks are just the shark picking up the bait and positioning it in its mouth. The usual 30-yard run can then be expected before the shark pauses, turns the bait head on, and swims away.

Let the line tighten exactly as I described in the earlier section on float-fishing. A bait that floats a little way off the seabed can really be attractive to a porbeagle. Use a little polystyrene for this, but only enough to add some buoyancy – you don't want the bait 5m (15ft) off the bottom. It works best when the bait alternates between touching bottom and free-floating.

With a clean seabed or one where the rough ground is made up of fine boulders and little weed growth, you've no problem as such in playing the shark. In the vicinity of rough, jagged reefs and rock overlaps you will obviously lose many fish when they take to the sanctuary of such places and break the line. If you want to ledger in such places, I'd suggest using heavy tackle: 20-kg (50-lb) class as a first choice, really applying early pressure to keep the sharks away from the reef. The largest porbeagles will fall to this technique early in the season. Likewise, in very deep water where large fish hug the bottom, once hooked they will need to be fought towards the surface, and rod pressure must be maximized to lift them.

When the sharks are on the surface and freely swimming around the boat, you can simply toss them a bait – even select the fish you want to hook. When they are moody they may leave a deadbait that sinks downward, even when free-lined. Free-lined live fish may be ignored because of the close proximity of the boat and crew. When this occurs it's worth trying one of the floating baits discussed in Chapter 7. This should float fully and be left to drift away from the hull some 10m (30ft), then given a twitch with the rod. This is a deadly method and, when a shark swims close to investigate, a couple of twitches to make the bait simulate death throws can trigger instant acceptance. This is something to bear in mind when the sharks are with you but less than confident to feed.

When you have found a good feeding area and wish to return the following day, it may be worth leaving a buoy behind with a bag of rubby-dubby suspended underneath. This should obviously be a large and visible buoy – but *never* do this close to major shipping lanes, only in areas with little boat activity. The bag of mush mixed with larger fish sections is better placed in a fine-meshed steel box. This does not guarantee that sharks will stay in the vicinity, but it does keep the smell lane intact and often the first run comes in minutes rather than hours the next day.

Instead of continuing to catch unwanted baitfish all day to keep those important vibrations in the water, you can make up a couple of drop lines. These are short pieces of rope, say 8m (25ft) long, with a 1-kg (2-lb) weight tied to the end. You pass small lengths of stainless-steel wire at intervals through the braid of the rope. Double one of the ends back to join with the other by twisting with pliers. Short lengths of 20-kg (50-lb) mono are tied to a loop made in the end of the wire. A 1/0 hook is tied to the mono. Live mackerel and other baitfish can be hooked onto these and lowered over the side where they will swim well for some time. Half-a-dozen mackerel is enough.

CHAPTER 9

Drift Fishing

Drift fishing for sharks was at one time considered the best method to locate these wandering fish consistently. The reason was that so little was known of the porbeagle's life-style that anglers and skippers could not make an educated guess as to their location. The majority of drift lines were cast where reports of big fish biting off anglers' lines or damaging nets had been made. Naturally, some success was achieved purely because of the mileage covered. Sooner or later a holding area would be found, and the drift became a permanent one.

The results of this technique were misinterpreted: in reality anglers were locating pockets of shark that had become territorial for a short period over a certain piece of ground. If the crews of these drifting boats had scrutinized their catches, they would have realized that 90 per cent of the drift was wasted effort – the same closely defined areas consistently produced all the runs.

However, developing the drift technique is a means of locating sharks when they are thinly spread after a storm or it is early in the season, when few fish are present in the feeding grounds. An effective drift should be slow. Too often, wind and tide working in the same direction create conditions where the boat moves far too fast. These are the worst conditions for making the chum trail work efficiently: most chum stays around and under the

boat, and may even be behind the boat's drift. Your chances of attracting sharks in this way are severely restricted.

To slow the boat down, it is possible to tow large buckets or garbage cans with some of their bases cut out. There are purpose-built drogues, but I've no personal experience of these. However, what worries me is the lines that connect these water-brakes to the boat. These take some time to retrieve and they most certainly create problems when fighting fish. A more reliable way of reducing speed on the drift is by incorporating a weight on the anchor rope – obviously without the anchor. I've seen skippers use sacks filled with pebbles and flat blocks cast from concrete with an eye set in them. These work well over clean ground but are of no use over mixed and rough ground. You can, of course, use the boat's engine to combat the tide, but this is costly and keeps an interested shark at a distance.

Worse conditions occur when there is no wind and the tide is slack. A lack of water movement sees the chum poorly spread, and the loss of wind causes the boat to remain stationary, with little ground effectively covered.

WHEN AND WHERE TO DRIFT

Ideal conditions are either wind against tide or wind sideways on to the tide. When

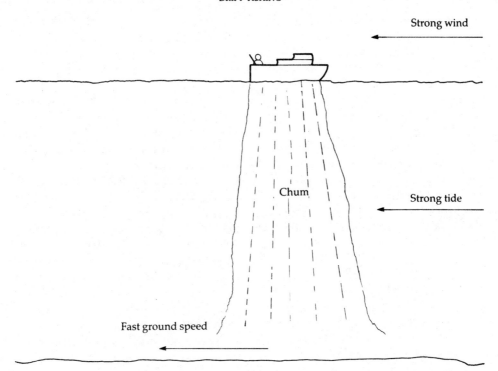

Strong wind

Strong tide

Chum

Fast ground speed

Figure 31: Chum-trail pattern when drift of boat is fast due to combined wind and tide

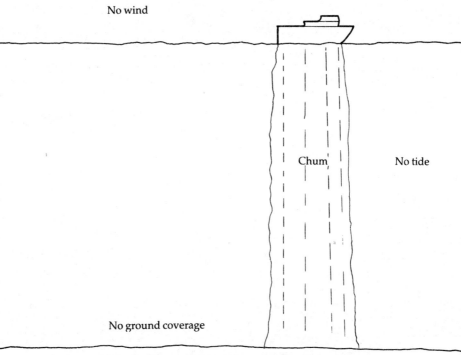

No wind

No tide

Chum

No ground coverage

Figure 32: Chum-trail pattern when no wind or tide is evident

the wind holds the boat against the tide, the boat barely moves, but the tide releases the chum scent much as we saw when anchored. The scent trail searches the water a long way from the boat. Equally good is a wind at a sideways angle to the flowing tide. The chum will still search downtide, but also to the side that faces the oncoming wind. The boat takes a diagonal course between wind and tide, and it's the angle of the boat that widens the scent lane a little more.

This diagonal travel applies whenever the wind and tide come from different angles. For instance, if the wind is southerly and the tide south-west, the angle of the boat will be south by south-west facing, but travelling in a north-easterly direction. If a northerly wind pushes the boat southerly, and the tide is running from the east, the travel of the boat will be to the south-west, and so on.

Knowing this helps us sort out the best times to drift certain areas when corresponding tides and winds offer the best combinations. As the factors of tides and wind directions change through the day, so too will your drift. When setting a pattern of balloons into a very fast tide-run, remember that the chum slick will not fall deep for a considerable distance. The furthest two baits set the deepest may not be in the actual slick. When wind strength increases past, say a five, and the boat drifts quickly, the scent trail will stay near the surface, perhaps only 10m (30ft) deep, 70m (75yds) from the boat. In these circumstances, set the balloons shallower. Also, when wind and tide together keep the chum directly below the boat, it's clear that shark are more likely to fall to the baits close to the boat.

When drift fishing, you need as much fresh dubby as possible. I stick to the

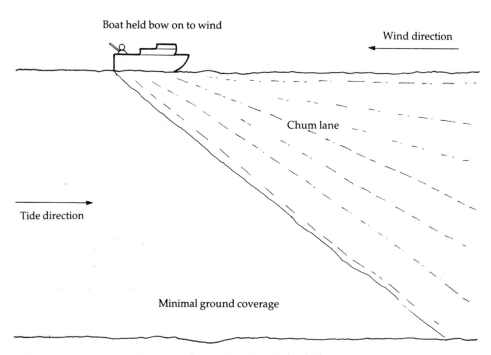

Boat held bow on to wind

Wind direction

Chum lane

Tide direction

Minimal ground coverage

Figure 33: Chum pattern when wind and tide oppose

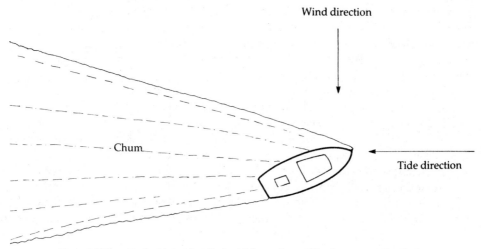

Wind direction

Tide direction

Chum

Figure 34: Chum trail widens when the boat takes a diagonal line between wind and tide

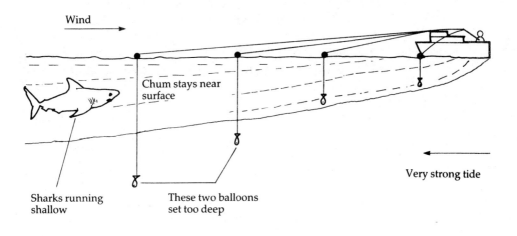

Wind

Chum stays near surface

Very strong tide

Sharks running shallow

These two balloons set too deep

Figure 35: Chum pattern in relation to balloon depth in fast tide-run

81

pattern of bags as described in Chapter 6, but continually freshen the bags. It follows that, with the extra amount of water being covered and any sideways motion of the chum by the wind, the strength of smell will be a little weaker than when at anchor.

The grounds I like to drift are principally the edges of reefs that have a lateral tide, either with the bait deep below the thermocline in the early months of the season or above the thermocline as the summer reaches a peak. Other good areas are the deeper breaks in a submerged reef that can be followed using the wind, tide, and sounder or across major drop-offs along the reef or natural gutters.

A drift designed to allow baits to traverse the incline of a sandbank can be fruitful, especially in summer when the

sharks use these banks to surprise baitfish. These drop-offs, when possible, should be drifted their full length. Continually crossing them at an angle reduces productive time.

You don't necessarily need ground feature for successful drift fishing. Locate the current lines (as we discussed earlier) and ascertain the side carrying the warmer water; this is a reliable place to drift. When fishing very deep water that causes problems when anchoring, I still employ the bags of dubby but use more chopped fish that sinks to all depths and encourages the sharks upwards.

For inshore drift fishing along shallow reefs and clean, sandy banks, I continue to use balloons to suspend the bait, and pattern the depth as before. Several bal-

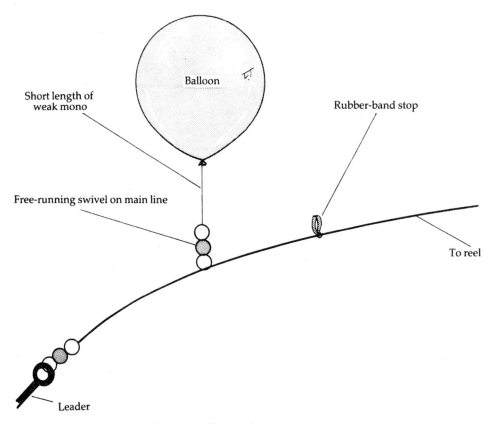

Figure 36: Balloon attachment for fast tide-run

loons are difficult to control when the boat is drifting in an indecisive way. I prefer only three balloons as a maximum. This cuts down on tangles as both the balloons and boat take on different angles. It's not unknown on days when the wind continually changes for the boat to go almost full circle and the balloons to stay still. I still prefer to use lead to keep the baits straight down from the balloon, but choose the spiral leads that attach to the upper leader – these offer less resistance to the tide, being more streamlined in shape.

I also use the free-spinning swivel jammed by a rubber band to attach the balloon via a piece of weak breaking-strain mono, although this depends on the weight of the bait being used. I like the freedom of the swivel; this allows the balloon to spin with the tide without the line twisting – otherwise the end tackle remains the same.

In deeper water, the baits are set deeper to find the feeding band. I usually set the furthest about 20m (70ft) down, the second at 15m (50ft), the third goes at 10m (30ft), and the inner balloon at about 6m (20ft). This is only a generalization. If you prefer, make the setting shallower or deeper as the day progresses. On brighter days it's again the deeper baits that invariably find the shark. Surface-set baits take fish when there is some cloud cover or rain clouds.

When bites are few and far between (or non-existent) it helps to retrieve a metre or so of line occasionally, then slowly release it back to its original position. This lifts the bait in the water and can interest a close-cruising shark. Incidentally, any takes tend to come as the bait is being trotted back to the original position – only rarely as the bait begins to lift, which you might have expected.

When the drift is gentle with an average tide, I often free-line a live mackerel. This

swims in a provocative manner a metre or so under the surface. The weight of the trace and leader ensures that the bait does not become too energetic. When they do show an increase in activity, it's a sure sign there's a major predator in the area – they can feel or sense their presence.

A porbeagle's take is not very dramatic. As already mentioned, the livebait starts to swim in an uneasy manner and darts from side to side. The shark comes in at speed, taking the mackerel either whole or sideways in its jaws, depending on the bait's size. The shark's impetus is maintained for 20–30yds, then the shark stops to turn or swallow the bait, and the strike is made as described before.

Sometimes, if the shark approaches from underneath the bait, its forward motion will bring it to the surface where, as it turns, it may cause a definite bulge in the surface water or actually break clear of the surface showing either its tail as it changes direction or both dorsal and tail as it arcs over to dive deeper. The observant angler will see this happen before any line is taken from the spool.

Another indication of a take is a slack line. When the livebait is swimming freely, its own movements and that of the boat's drift tend to keep the line fairly tight. When a shark hits the bait and comes towards the boat, the line falls slack. Again, the observant angler will see this happen and be forewarned of a run.

On a faster drift, when the wind and tide are the same way, I use a weighted deadbait. This is almost a slow troll and proves very effective. I usually try to fish four baits with a different weight of lead on each to vary the depth at which they fish. The method of setting up the bait so that it swims on an even keel (without spinning) is the same as the system I use for powered trolling. This is described in the following chapter, as is the pattern for the four baits.

Deadbait can be given increased life by removing the backbone so that the body becomes more flexible. I've also tried filleting the bait, removing the whole backbone and leaving the flanks attached to the head. This gives a most life-like swimming action.

With a light lead, the bait sits only a metre or so under the surface. Often the shark can be seen with its fin out of the water advancing on the bait. It will dive out of sight some 6m (20ft) or so from the bait. This is the beginning of the shark's attacking run.

During any fishing session, whether at anchor or drifting, the line between the rod tip and bait will continually slacken and re-tighten. This is more noticeable on a fast drift with the line stretching under the strain then releasing as the boat moves to the whim of tide and wind. To avoid a potential weak spot (where the line sits inside the tip ring or roller) I prefer to release a few centimetres of line every half hour or so. This prevents a permanent rub on a small section of line. The water colour and cloud conditions have less importance with moving baits. The smell of the chum and the moving bait encourage the shark upward towards the surface. Whether the sky is cloudless or filled with light-obscuring cloud matters little – your chances of success remain almost the same. On days when the sun is bright and the water clear, a faster drift is advantageous. On dark days, when the water is less clear, more success is likely if the drift is slow. I tend to set the baits deeper in clear water and slightly shallower in coloured water. I can't really identify a pattern that suggests surface-swimming baits are superior to deeper baits. It's an even chance as to which will be taken on the day.

Generally, the longer the drift, the more chance you have of finding sharks, not only because you cover more ground but also because the chum has a real opportunity to work efficiently. When I've been in deep water where ground feature has been relatively unimportant, I've experienced drifts of over 20 miles (30km) and almost always seen one or two fish. When drifting inshore between reefs or through natural gutters, runs may be only a few hundred metres long before the engines are needed to take you back to your original starting position. I dislike this style of drifting – it loses so much time but is, sometimes, the only option you have.

I prefer to motor back slowly, with the chum sacks still in the water. This maintains the unbroken scent lane, even if it is a little weak. The bags should be replaced whenever possible with new ones with fresh contents when re-starting the actual drift. I also like to add freshly chopped fish over the side at the start of a new drift. This falls to the seabed, where some of it lodges in depressions, etc., and other pieces wander downtide. The best system is the tin of blood and pulped fish that continually trickles its contents over the side. This ensures an unbroken smell lane for the shark to follow.

CHAPTER 10

Experimental Fishing

TROLLING – THE POTENTIAL

In many parts of Europe and on the American continent, the use of artificial lures, deadbaits, and livebaits trolled behind powered boats is a reliable and consistent method of capturing large, predatory fish. However, in areas that are well frequented by porbeagles, capturing this shark on trolled baits is a rare occurrence. Much of the problem stems from the high average speeds needed to work a lure fast enough to attract the billfishes, tuna, etc., that are the main targets of such methods. Speeds are between 7 and 15km/h (4 and 8kn) – far too fast for porbeagles that, although capable of reaching these speeds with ease, prefer to take food in a more leisurely manner.

When in Australia, I've trolled lures from boats with some success for a range of species, and I felt fairly confident when I tried this method in British waters. I was to be disappointed, however, for having trolled artificial kona heads, deadbaits, and livebaits over what must now run into several hundred miles, I've yet to experience a hook-up. On the other hand, a group of anglers fishing the west coast of Ireland a few years ago did succeed in hooking and landing porbeagles on trolled mackerel deadbaits. Speeds in the region of 7km/h (4kn) were found to be successful.

I've had a porbeagle fin follow my boat (which was travelling at 3.5km/h (2kn)

towing mackerel deadbait for about 275m (300yd)), but when the shark eventually dived, the anticipated run failed to materialize. In a sense, a deadbait or livebait fished from a rapidly drifting boat is a trolled bait. I've had many fish like this, but would never consider this method to be trolling: to troll you must be under power and making way.

Why, then, is the technique of trolling so poorly appreciated by the porbeagle? There are several reasons. First are travelling speeds. Having talked to a few anglers who have tried this method, but without success, I found that they all seem intent on working the bait too quickly. The average speed employed appears to be about 11km/h (6kn). Usually two or three baits are used, fishing a pattern 45m (50yd), 70m (75yd), and 90m (100yd) behind the boat, the furthest lure being in the centre. These lures are fished from rods that are simply positioned on the stern of the boat and tied down with rope. None of these anglers report hook-ups, runs, or even visual sightings of porbeagles when fishing in this manner.

Secondly, although we already know that porbeagles react well to the vibrations given off by fish in distress, the swimming motion – however powerful – from a trolled deadbait or lure is going to be confounded by the turbulence of the boat's propeller. When fishing in the clear waters off Europe and off the east coast of

America, this turbulence actually brings shark to the boat – or at least into the vicinity, when eyesight takes over. In the more cloudy waters of the British Isles, it's doubtful that the shark would actually see the lure or bait until it was almost upon it. If the shark should home in on propeller turbulence, it would probably cruise past the bait, completely oblivious of it. In such conditions it would be prudent to employ a couple of surface lures that skip on the water (such as Japanese birds) and fish both of these with the deadbait well back from the boat at a distance of at least 90m (100yd) where the noise from the engines is less.

It's interesting to note that the west coast of Ireland (where some success with trolled baits for porbeagles was achieved) has very clear water with excellent visibility. This must allow an obvious silhouette for the shark to follow and attack.

One of the most common and elementary mistakes is to pay no attention to the

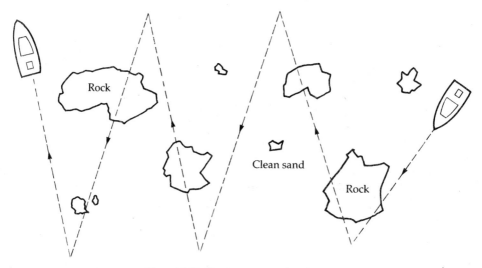

Figure 37: Trolling pattern over selected ground

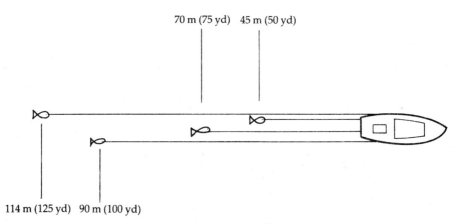

70 m (75 yd)   45 m (50 yd)

114 m (125 yd)   90 m (100 yd)

Figure 38: Four-bait staggered-trolling pattern

area to be trolled. Even though the boat will cover a large amount of ground, if there are no porbeagles your time will, of course, be wasted. It is of no use to push out into deeper water trolling for 15 or 20 miles in a dead straight line; it is clearly better to note where recent shark captures have been made and troll over this area.

Ground composition can help enormously. The places to try are rocky reefs where sharks are used to rising in the water to take pollack and mackerel. Also favourable are deeper trenches, particularly along the edges of sandbanks. Pay particular attention to water currents that meet and divide. Locating these, and working the warm water side with lures, may pay dividends. When a promising piece of ground has been found, use a zigzag pattern to criss-cross over it continuously; straight-line runs are the least productive. Keep the boat's turns wide to avoid any of the bait lines crossing and becoming tangled.

The patterns of the lures we troll need to be better understood. I feel it's a mistake to have the longest lines in the centre, as most people seem to prefer. I usually only fish three lines, although four is all right with care. Lures fished from rods leant over the stern are called flat lines. I set the two outer lines at a distance of 114m

(125yd) and 90m (100yd) behind the boat. These outer baits can be either large and heavy, fishing deep, or light and small, skipping on the surface. The two inner lines should be baited differently to the outer lines: if the outer lines employ a large, heavy bait, the inner lines should be set up with a lighter bait that breaks the surface. This should fish at 45m (50yd) and 70m (75yd) rear of the stern. The outside lines could employ artificial lures that bob on the surface, thus creating a disturbance to attract the sharks.

In many parts of the world, the outside lines are fished on outriggers set out from the boat. These widen the pattern, allowing up to five lines to be fished in a comfortable manner and improving the display. Unfortunately, I'm not aware of any British boats that have this facility. John Mitchell, of Aberaeron, Wales, and I experimented with home-built outriggers on his boat and ironed out most of the original problems. The line from the rod has an elastic band looped over it. I make three loose coils of line by wrapping it round my four fingers; the rubber band then goes through the centre of the coils. The elastic band has both loops placed over a spring clip. The clip is situated on a string which runs the full length of the outrigger. The string runs through two

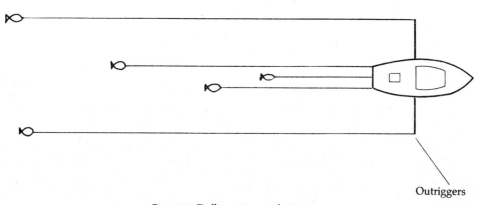

Outriggers

Figure 39: Trolling pattern with outriggers

eyes on the outrigger to make a pulley system akin to that of a flagpole. The clip carrying the baited line is run up to the tip of the outrigger. The elastic band takes the full strain of the trolled bait, but breaks when a fish is hooked.

In more lively seas, when sizeable baits are being used, you may need to add a second elastic band to spread the load of boat and tidal surge – this can momentarily overload the band, which breaks. It pays to release the outrigger lines to their fishing position before the flat lines: this saves time, tangles, and temper. Flat lines that rely on the reel's drag to hold the bait when actually fishing can be used in almost any sea. However, in rough weather when varying amounts of pressure are imposed on the line, I prefer to hold the rod. When they're not in your hands, always have the rods tied down with a strong rope to avoid losing them over the side.

The patterns we can use with trolled baits are endless. Trolling for porbeagle is only in its infancy, so much is just an educated guess. However, from the start I felt that the most likely approach to yield success would come from having two

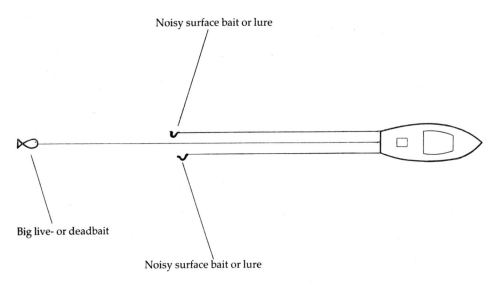

Noisy surface bait or lure

Big live- or deadbait

Noisy surface bait or lure

Figure 40: Predator shadowing baitfish-trolling pattern

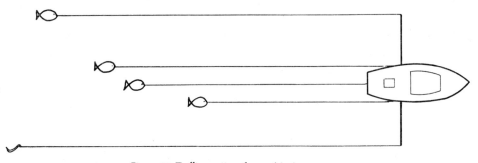

Figure 41: Trolling pattern for persistent manoeuvre

outside lures (or small light baitfish) creating noise and disturbance on the water. This should be worked in conjunction with an inside bait, set more heavily and deeper. This bait should be at least 1 kg (2 lb) in size. It imitates a medium-sized predatory fish shadowing a school of smaller baitfish – a completely natural target for the porbeagle.

Teasers, or daisy chains, are groups of dead baitfish rigged on ropes and lines without hooks to simulate a free-swimming shoal of baitfish. This works well enough, but setting up such lines is time-consuming. I now choose to use artificial imitations that are quicker and cleaner and need less attention when fishing, yet they provide the same degree of attraction.

I use US artificial mackerel imitations. You can use any number, from just a couple to as many as eight or more. For very slow trolling, these artificials can be placed about 60cm (2ft) apart; for faster speeds, I prefer a gap of 1m (3ft). Close attention to the teasers must be given as

a shark may attack these if they are left in the water when a fish is sighted in the boat's wake. When a change of course will be needed on a regular basis, a staggered V-pattern allows up to five baits to be fished without tangles when the boat turns and gives slack line.

Surface baits down to a depth of 8m (25ft) may not always provide the answer. Using a downrigger to hold a fish bait at a certain depth may prove effective over lifting sandbanks and the edges of rocky reefs. In addition, if the thermocline can be found and a bait positioned in this band of even-temperature water by the use of a down rigger, this would be a great advantage at certain times of the year.

It's customary to use the boat's power to set the hook in areas where predatory fish are regularly caught on trolled lures and baits. This should not be necessary with porbeagle that turn away after eating the bait, taking line from the reel. If the drag is set correctly, the fish should either hook itself or it can be hooked by the

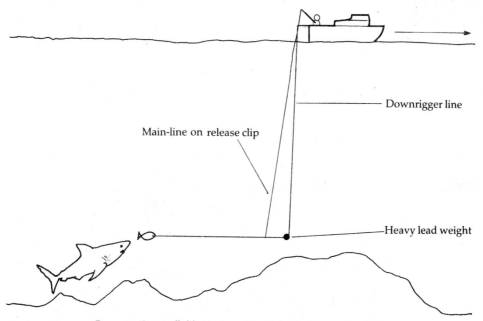

Figure 42: Deep-trolled bait using a downrigger for deep-running shark

Downrigger line

Main-line on release clip

Heavy lead weight

angler as the shark is running — providing the speed of run is not too great (this is because trolling speeds are slow).

To set up a dead mackerel for use as a trolling bait, you need a normal wire trace and hook, a short length of stainless-steel wire, and a drilled lead bullet. I place the single hook just to the rear of the gills so that the hook's eye comes level with the front of the lips when the hook is in

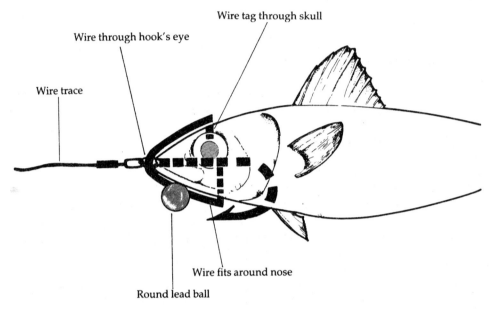

Figure 43: Method of hook-mounting a trolled deadbait

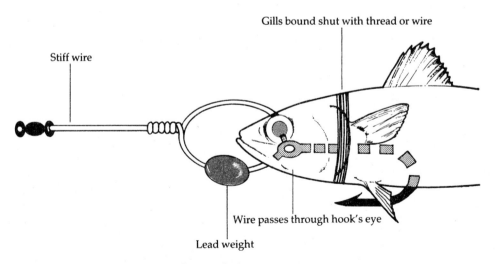

Figure 44: Alternative hook-mounting for trolled deadbait

position. The stainless-steel wire (some 18 gauge in size) is bent at the middle until it fits the snout of the mackerel when the mouth is closed. The wire should have enough length to allow two tags to be bent at right angles to the main stem. The upper one is inserted downwards through the bone between the eyes. The lower one goes through the hook's eye. Now thread this on the lead weight and check that it sits in the cavity created by the lower jaw. The second bend is made in this wire so that it punctures the lower jaw below the eyes. Push this home. Finally, wrap either elasticated cotton or copper wire of a fine diameter around the mackerel's snout, and wire. This system is preferable to having a long length of heavy, stiff wire leading the mackerel, as depicted below right.

It is necessary to remove the bait's tail fin as this reduces any tendency for the bait to spin under motion. I've trolled distanced up to 25 miles (40km) at speeds of 5.5km/h (3kn) with no line twist and, because of the lead weight (which acts as a keel), the swimming action is superb when the backbone is removed. By placing the wire through the hook's eye, the weight of the trolled bait is taken by the strong bone that lies between the baitfish's eyes. I bind its mouth closed to prevent the passage of water, which would destroy the swimming action and cause excessive drag.

A slowly trolled livebait should be a deadly method when used in the areas associated with porbeagles. Presentation should be on a bridle rig as described before. This is a slow-trolling method – speeds need to be kept about 3.5km/h (2kn) to avoid killing the livebait.

I've already mentioned artificial lures used in conjunction with deadbaits but I'm sure that, when some effort has been put into experimentation with kona heads, knuckle heads, birds, etc., these will become a successful method for taking porbeagles. I've already tried these frequently in British waters. However, problems with this style of fishing arise from an almost total lack of knowledge about this form of angling by otherwise excellent charter skippers. Few are willing to experiment with new methods when older systems still produce excellent results. Much of the trolling I've done has been from relatively small craft of under 5.5m (18ft) with one other companion. This is necessary to maximize time, but the weather also needs to be perfect for a boat of this size to work far out to sea – it's a vicious circle, but well worth pursuing. Several porbeagles have been hooked on large, chromed pirks worked over wrecks with the boat on drift. This could be just the sort of place to persist with deep-trolled artificial lures, such as a large spoon or large, artificial squid.

In the warmer, clearer seas of the world, the brighter green, yellow, and red colours work well during the day, but I doubt this will be the case in the colder waters of the British Isles. We must bear in mind the lack of detail when a shark views a prospective meal from below. We need to enhance the silhouette. Black and blue are likely to be the most effective colours, although red would also be worth trying as it is the darkest of the warm colours. When fishing in warmer waters, the brighter colours tend to be taken on days when light levels are high. Darker tones are preferred at dusk, dawn, and when light levels are low.

Many trolling lures carry the option of holding a cyalume light stick for extra appeal. I've little real experience of these but would feel confident about using them when a surface lure breaks the water. During dusk and dawn this would simulate the plankton explosion as the water is disturbed by feeding fish. Plastic squid can also be used as this type of lure. Some of these are up to 45cm (18in) long and, with the addition of a light stick, would be a good imitation of a real squid's fluorescent skin particles as they change colour under the water.

Some of the larger metal spoons fished over rough ground or reefs, or as part of the lure pattern, are certainly a possibility. Experience with other fish suggests that these would be effective when light levels are good – the light reflects off the lure's chrome finish, which will attract the shark as it homes in. Small, plastic squid skirts or muppets are not a good proposition fished on their own but, when placed over a deadbait so that the plastic fingers swim to add movement, they may help to trigger a reaction from a half-interested shark. I often fish one of these above the bait, say 23cm (9in) up from the snout of the bait. This gives added movement, and simulates a baitfish chasing a small squid.

The addition of a small length of chamois leather, well soaked in pilchard oil and bound to the hook on a trolled lure, is used by many anglers. If this helps your confidence, it's worth considering; personally I doubt its validity. The constant water action past the lure will quickly wash any scent sway, so its actual effectiveness will be measured in minutes.

Many times, when fishing baits under balloons and using chum, you get a shark that perpetually fins in the surface water yet refuses to go down for one of the baits. These are the fish that may well take an artificial lure. The knack would be to buoy the anchor off while retrieving the balloon baits. If the bait's added movement still doesn't interest the shark, then try a quick change to a kona head or other trolled lure paid out from the stern, the engine (under light revs) taking the boat away from the shark. It's important to leave the dubby bags in the water and to steer a course to come round in a wide circle until the lure trails well behind the boat, either close by the shark or over the area where it was last seen. Never steer a course straight for a shark – you will only spook it and force it down. With minimal power and noise, and using a shallow approach, it's amazing how close you can get to a finning shark.

Large plugs are another possibility: many modern ones are well made from good materials and capable of withstanding an hour in a shark's jaws. A mixture of deep divers and shallow floaters are the best combination. If a big fin broaches the surface when you are at anchor, and it adopts the common zigzag search pattern yet refuses to dive for the baits, there is the possibility of casting large spinners and plugs into its path. I remember, many years ago, two anglers fishing from a small boat in southern Ireland who obtained a hook-up on a shark on a large rapala plug that had been cast as the shark cruised in the slick. The fish, I believe, broke away but this proves the technique's viability. Tackle would need to be re-designed for this method. A rod 3m (10ft) long with some flexibility in its tip but with vast reserves of power in the butt for pressure lifting would be the basis for experimentation. I'd use a light-weight multiplier holding 360–450m (400–500yd) of 9–13.5-kg (20–30-lb) line. The wire trace would need to be only a metre or so long as the shark would inevitably be lip hooked. A short cast should be used with an abrasive length of 45-kg (100-lb) mono, and a swivel between the mono and wire trace. Large spinners would pose no problems in casting, but plugs may have to be floated away with the tide.

In America, offshore spinning rods are used for smaller predators, but I do not know of this being tried specifically for sharks. Long, slim pirks, with an added plastic skirt to disguise the hook, have been taken by porbeagles over wrecks, as already mentioned. Chances of takes are favourable if these are cast to cruising fish.

CHAPTER 11

Light-Tackle Fishing

Light-tackle fishing is a valid method for catching porbeagles, except when using lines that are too fine. Lines with a breaking strain of less than 5.5 kg (12 lb) impose far too little pressure on the fish for it to be subdued by rod alone; instead, the boat is used from the outset to minimize the distance the shark can run. I've heard of several instances where relatively small blue and porbeagle sharks have been lured to within close proximity of the boat, have had a mackerel bait lowered to them and, when they have taken the bait, are not allowed to run. They are held by the double line and strong wire trace, and are hence quickly gaffed. This is, quite simply, cheating. The reel may be loaded with 2-kg (4-lb) line, but it never leaves the spool. The boat is manoeuvred to within gaffing range of the bemused fish, which is simply gaffed aboard.

The use of a double line is allowed by international rules – you can use a length of reel line doubled and attached to the main leader to allow more pressure to be exerted on a fish when it is brought to the side of the boat by an angler using light line. However, the gross inefficiency of very light tackle can be demonstrated by the fact that many shark hooked up on lines of 4 kg (8 lb) and less actually take a second bait while being played. Obviously, the fish is unaware of the pressure supposedly being imposed by the angler. In reality, the angler equipped with such

light line cannot afford to let the shark run a great length of line. The pressure exerted by the water on the line's surface as a total mass is more than enough to break it. Wire traces, swivels, and the length of line all create drag and increase pressure.

I know of two similar light-tackle incidents: in both the sharks ate the bait and continued to swim towards the stern of the boat. The crew watched the oncoming balloon while the angler retrieved line. As the shark cruised slowly past the stern, a member of the crew gaffed the fish. At no time was the rod bent – an abhorrent thing to do. Furthermore, too many sharks break the line and end up towing metres of line and the hook and trace. Any sports-person does their best to keep instances like this to an absolute minimum.

It is also important to clarify the boat's exact duty and the consequences of its manoeuvring. If a large fish should run, under its own steam, away from the boat so reducing the amount of line on the angler's reel to around 90m (100yd), the motor should be used to reduce the distance between the angler and fish. There is an obvious need for this: if a fish is capable of running all the line off, then a break is inevitable – the fish would probably die from dragging so much line behind it. It take the angler's skill to subdue such a fish, but the skipper's essential skill is, at the same time, not to be overlooked. In these situations the fish should be shared between the angler and the skipper. This is a different form of light-line fishing from that described earlier. Perhaps in the future some demarcation of this joint technique from the standard stand-up or sit-down static fights (which are currently the norm) will be enforced.

Real light-line skills come into play with lines over 6 kg (12 lb) test. The angler now has an outfit that can impose pressure on the shark. The shark is also aware that it is in danger, and fights hard and long. When large fish are involved, there is a balance between the conservative use of the angler's energy and skills with rod and reel, and the wild intelligence of a predatory fish. To succeed, the angler must sap the fish's energy.

For purposes of clarification, 12-, 20- and 30-class tackle are light. I personally rarely use the 6 kg (12 lb) except when I know there is a high chance of catching small pups. Good anglers admire a line-to-catch ratio of 10:1; in other words, a 90-kg (200-lb) shark on 10-kg (20-lb) line. In practice, a ratio of 5:1 is good and something to be proud of.

This type of light-tackle fishing needs to be practised by no more than two anglers on one boat. If a larger group are willing to sacrifice fishing time while a big fish is being played (perhaps for several hours) then this is fine. However, this is rarely the case. Anglers generally expect value for money. Heavy tackle is therefore the first choice to minimize fight time and to give everyone a chance of shark.

When using lines down to 6-kg (12-lb) test, I refuse to use a permitted length of double line – this is unnecessary. I tie my reel line direct to the top swivel of the leader and fish as normal. I generally tie the rubber band and balloon to this top swivel, content to fish shallow. Deep dropping and light lines do not go together. I fish no deeper than 10m (30ft). When this depth is required, I dislike using a rubber

band half-hitched onto the line. When the balloon is tied to the rubber band, the point of wear and abrasion is concentrated, and the weaker-than-normal line may not take it. I use a fine rubber band half-hitched to the line purely as a stop, but use a small, free-running swivel as before. The length of light mono that goes between the swivel and balloon should be reduced to no more than 2 kg (4 lb). This gives the swivel some freedom and avoids line scuff. The finer rubber band goes through the rod rings without problems.

Few anglers realize how different fighting big fish is on light lines compared to using 23-kg (50-lb) class and above. Many anglers seem to suffer from a mental block that stops them letting their quarry run line from the reel. In practice, this actually assists the angler using lighter tackle – once more, it's the friction of water pressure on the line that helps. The more line you have out from the reel, the greater the pressure build-up on the line. This increases when the shark changes direction, creating a wide belly in the line. This is the critical moment with ultra-light gear. It's now that poor knots and line abrasions part – with a sickening twang.

Reel clutches must be in first-class working order, and set to give line easily when called upon to do so. Lever drag reels are very precise for this type of fishing but, contrary to popular belief, you're at no great disadvantage when using a properly maintained star drag. You often read of less experienced big-fish anglers who say that under no circumstances should you alter the drag pressure or manually assist the reel with thumb or finger pressure.

I've been privileged to watch anglers I greatly respect battle with big fish. The very best of these have a sixth sense – an inbuilt feeling for the sport – and they all add extra drag when needed by applying the ball of the thumb. This ability to cal-

94

culate exactly how much pressure the line is under is the mark of an experienced angler. The drag must invariably be adjusted as needed when a large fish runs several hundred metres from the boat. As the line level falls, so the drag pressure is increased. Drag pressure should be eased a little as every hundred metres of line is lost. This should not be increased until plenty of line has been retrieved. To gain line, the thumb is used to hold the spool solidly while you pump to gain line. This thumb pressure should be applied very gently. The line you release under your thumb should not be allowed to get hot or skid, as this will weaken it.

The angler using heavier gear can hold the fish firmly, helping to reduce the shark's strength. The drag can also be set heavier, making the fish work hard for any line gained. This applies less to the light-tackle angler, who needs to work appreciably harder to subdue the shark. The fish should be allowed to run against a sensible reel drag until plenty of line is out. As soon as the fish slows, the angler must pump hard to regain line and keep this up until the fish needs line as a new run develops. Letting the shark cruise around with little rod pressure exerted on it, only serves to give it a rest. The angler is not always given a choice but, where possible, fight the fish at a distance. This will exploit line drag and also give you and the skipper time to manoeuvre.

One blessing is that most light-tackle sharks prefer to fight on the surface. Their runs will be longer than normal because of the light drag but few, fortunately, sound. Some still head underneath the boat, so care is needed to avoid the line chaffing on the hull or fouling the propeller.

When a shark is ready for landing or sat underneath the boat, release the drag to a nil setting and avoid over-runs by holding light thumb pressure. Sharks in this situation can either dive straight down or pick a new direction and run fast. If this happens, let them get well away from the boat before you begin to replay them. If a shark should sound and hug the seabed, use the boat's engine to reposition yourself away from the shark to shallow the angle of the reel line towards the shark. Light tackle in a straight up-and-down pull against the shark is simply no match – you must bear in mind that it takes more force to move a static spool of line than it does a spool that is already moving and giving line. In turn, when the weight of a shark is directly below the angler's rod tip, the rod will be set well into its fighting curve and the line will be fully taught: you have no give in the rod or line to allow a margin of safety should the fish suddenly move. When the shark does move, the extra pressure cannot be soaked up and, as the force needed to move the static reel spool begins to build up, the line may well part.

The procedure for landing fish is as before: the hook trace and leader remain the same as with heavy gear. It's these that take the strain when a shark is being tailed or, if you must, gaffed.

RODS

Even today, tackle for light-line fishing is very much a compromise, but make do and mend has never been a sound basis on which to develop good technique. The average length for a boat rod should be somewhere between 2 and 2.3m (6 and 7ft). More far-sighted companies add on a few more centimetres. This is suitable for heavy-line work, say 30 class and upwards, but for lighter-line classes I prefer rods with a full length of 2.5m (8ft). This extra length, coupled with a forgiving tip, helps to protect light lines from sudden stress. The added length also allows for more control when the shark approaches the boat.

The butt section needs to have lifting strength when the whole rod locks under power. Alloy tube of aircraft strength is acceptable, but not wood or chromed brass – these materials are heavy and outdated (see Chapter 14 for details of the rod's overall construction). These rods bend a great deal and would benefit from light-weight rings that allow an element of flexibility. Some rings on modern rods are far too rigid for light-tackle work. Adding a roller tip ring offers no real advantage, but you must take care to select a ring that produces least line friction. Modern Fuji rings are hard to beat and are available worldwide. Spigot fittings of the standard male-into-female variety are not the best choice for this type of fishing. The tip section should lock onto the butt with an alloy nut and thread, preferably incorporating a well-aligned metal lug for exact tip positioning in relation to the butt.

Many modern rods from different companies end up with the reel seat out of line with the rings – keen light-tackle anglers should make an effort to construct their own rods. You can build them to suit your own needs and you can incorporate the very best and newly available materials and components.

REELS

A big 4/0 or 6/0 reel is not suitable for very light line. Instead, you should choose a modern, light-weight multiplier that gives a capacity of 550m (600yd) of 9-kg (20-lb) line or 180m (200yd) more of 5-kg (12-lb) line. For strength, this should be attached to the reel with a timber hitch and then packed onto the reel in touching turns for the first 180m (200yd). This forms a firm foundation for the rest of the line, which is the more likely to be used. Choose a spool with an alloy construction

and check this for true alignment. To do this, place chalk marks opposite each other on the rim of each spool end. Any misalignment will be seen when the spool is spun quickly.

Drag washers should be cleaned well in petrol, even when new. Use only graphite powder as a lubricant. Never leave the drag on when the reel is not in use as this flattens and compresses the washers. Aim to renew drag washers every two or three trips and after each battle with a big fish. Some manufacturers now produce good-quality, low-price lever drags. These give a shade more precision when you re-adjust the pressure. They can also be set to a finer degree of release because of the large overall size of the drag plates and washers. If there is a choice, I prefer reels with a solid-brass frame. Many modern reels are constructed around a graphite frame. Under load, these can sometimes distort, which reduces my confidence in this type of construction.

In my opinion, the best of the lever drags are the Penn International 12 and 20. In the cheaper range for 12 and 20 class, either the Daiwa LD50 or the Penn 40 GLS offer strength and reliability. This is backed up with a first-class spares' service when needed. Other makes may be equally reliable, but stories of burst spools, distorted frames, and a lack of spares make me cautious and slow to change.

In the star-drag category, nearly all my fish have come on an ABU 10,000c, and this remains my first choice. This company has perhaps the best spares' service, but little goes wrong with these tough reels. Always use the steady lugs and seat clamp as well as the standard reel seat for joining reel to rod. I've seen reels work loose from the seat fixture on many occasions when under load. This can be avoided by extra bracing. It's always important with any class of tackle to lay the line out neatly on the retrieve. This is essential with light line. Any bunching or multiple overlay can be disastrous when a fish wants to run.

LINE

Use only monofilament – my reasons for preferring this to braided line are given in Chapter 14. I use the harder, stiffer lines as these knot better and tend not to keep tightening when the knot is under stress, which can also eventually cause a break. Stiff lines are less prone to scratching and abrasion, and stretch less.

Some line stretch is essential for light-tackle fishing, but too much is a sign of weakness. Use good-quality brands, such as Ande, ABU Test, and Maxima. I also use Berkley Trilene for any 12-class work. These lines stretch a little and then lock, which is good, giving the angler some idea of the level of stress being imposed on the line.

LEADERS

I use commercial-grade 114-kg (250-lb) mono for the leader and then add a short, biting piece of wire. The leader needs to be 3–4m (10–12ft) long. All swivels should be 6/0 Berkleys or Sampos (or equivalents) except the upper swivel, to which the reel line is tied. This carries no weight and need only be a 4/0.

Being soft in comparison to the wire some other anglers prefer means that mono gives a better, more subtle feel to the fight through the rod. I also get more bites when using mono compared to wire. I'm sure that, when a shark takes the bait and lifts a little in the water, it feels the wire's extra weight and this increases its chances of dropping the bait. Wire must also stand out as a stark, black line when seen against the surface whereas mono

blends a little better with the surface background.

The biting piece should remain at around 1–1.3m (3–4ft) to give an overall length of leader and trace that does not exceed 4.6m (15ft). I use multi-strand wire between 204 and 272 kg (450 and 600 lb) test, not for the breaking strain but to combat the shark's teeth.

HOOKS

Hooks used are as normal, but I tend to choose a size smaller than I'd use on heavier gear. A 10/0 suits the 20 outfit and an 8/0 works well with the 12. These must be ultra-sharp, so I modify the barb by reducing its angle and depth. This aids the hook's penetration when the line comes tight.

Never be tempted to strike when using light line. This overloads the line (and possibly even the rod) and will lose fish. As before, let the line tighten into the shark and rely on this to sink the hook.

GENERAL TIPS

To avoid the excessive strain imposed by balloons on the light line when a shark dives with the bait, I not only use a weak piece of mono that will break between the swivel and the balloon due to water pressure, but I also prefer (on most occasions) to swap the balloon for a small, net cork. These give ample buoyancy for suspending the bait and trace and, usefully, create less drag when being pulled through the water. Small, cheap, and gaudily coloured plastic balls have the same function.

I prefer to use light-line tackle as a way of creating opportunity: when sharks are cruising round the boat, it's worthwhile just to lower the bait into the water, letting the sharks sort themselves out or actually choosing the fish you want to hook – dropping the bait on its nose as it swims past. This also reduces the worry of light gear being taken by a very large shark: no one really wants to tackle a 226-kg (500-lb) fish on 12-class tackle.

I always fish light gear shallow and near to the boat. I usually have two heavy outfits further out, with the two light outfits within 27m (30yd) of the stern. This also keeps more line on the reel for the initial run. In the right hands, 20 class is a good combination, capable of subduing very large fish. This can be fished deeper and further away from the boat.

CHAPTER 12

Shark Boats

The type of boat you use is important, not only in its design but also in its crew's ability and the quality of its basic equipment. Before you charter a boat, you should ask several questions. What experience of sharks does the skipper have? Does the skipper have a reliable and consistent reputation for their capture? It always pays off to stick with a skipper who knows the ground and sharks — this cuts down on wasted effort and time. Will there be a crew member on board? This is not necessary when members of your own party are well versed in handling big fish at the side of the boat, but problems arise when no such person is available and the skipper is needed to keep the motors running, and the stern and angler facing the fish.

Always raise the question of dubby. Good skippers provide this themselves, but some expect you to provide your own. In the same vein, check that mincing facilities, and so on, are available on board. Ideally, the dubby should be waiting for you as you board the boat. Don't settle for a mixing session when you arrive on the fishing grounds — it's your time the skipper is wasting. Check that quality hook baits will be available: even freshly frozen ones are better than having to go out in the hope of finding fresh bait on the way.

Make certain the gaffs and tailers aboard are up to the job. Twice I've been aboard so-called shark boats only to find the skipper had no tailer and produced a poor-quality gaff that would be hard pressed to hold even a small pup. Have nothing to do with a skipper who insists on keeping all the sharks — he'll sell them when you return to port. Except for large specimens that can be justifiably taken in for weighing (good publicity for the boat) they should all be returned immediately.

Essential though safety equipment may be to you, some boat-owners seem less than concerned with it. Make a point of asking exactly what safety equipment is on board. Good charter captains will answer politely; those who don't, I'd rather not go to sea with. Old life-jackets, out-of-date flares, radios that don't work, and unreliable engines are ingredients for disaster.

Once a price has been agreed on, make sure you know exactly what you'll get for your money. This saves much unpleasantness later. Many professional skippers now issue a contract that states their charges and services. This not only binds the skipper to providing those facilities but also binds you. Other than cancellation through bad weather, you must still pay if you fail to turn up.

In the preceding paragraphs I've deliberately painted a bad picture: most skippers are excellent seafarers, with quality boats and a genuine concern for your safety and enjoyment on the trip. A minority couldn't care less, and it's these I've tried to warn you against.

In areas where sharks are found close inshore, the boat's speed is of little consequence. When the ground to be fished lies well offshore, a boat with a poor turn of speed may see you steaming for three or four hours out – and the same for the return journey. Obviously, faster, higher-powered boats save time. What may be a cheaper price on a slower boat may cost you dear in actual fishing time.

What does the skipper ask of you? Most skippers respond best to anglers who are keen to fish. Beer-swilling parties are best left until the return to shore. Respect the boat and its equipment. Always use a bait-board for cutting and preparing baits, never the top of gunnels or some convenient seat or engine cover. Keep gear and tackle tidy or, preferably, stowed neatly away in the cabin. It must always be possible to travel the decks easily, either for fighting fish or in an emergency. At the end of a successful capture, any blood or slime should be washed from the decks to avoid slipping.

On the return trip, I always like to wash the boat off and clean things up. Some anglers presume the skipper accepts this as part of the job; I disagree, you made the mess so you clean it up. A little effort during the day sees things kept to a minimum anyway. Some boat-owners prefer to do this task themselves, but a little good public relations on your part works wonders for subsequent trips.

When four or more members in a party all want to fish, it's a sensible idea to organize a roster, taking it in turns to fight (you hope) the prolific shark. It's a sad fact of shark-fishing that, in a group of several, one angler may catch three while the others never see their balloons move.

Most shark anglers have their own tackle these days. If you're just starting out, however, and are feeling your way in the sport, you may prefer to hire some gear from the skipper. This can either be in excellent shape or just about seized solid. Check the drag on the reel works correctly and gives line on cue. Is there enough line on the spool? Make sure the reel is well clamped to the rod. Have a look to see that the rod rings are aligned and not bent out of shape. If a rod is fitted with roller rings, are these free or seized with corrosion? Are the knots that secure the reel line to the leader good? And the wire trace itself – does it show signs of corrosion and oxidization. If so, ask for a fresh one. Check the hook is not badly pitted with rust and, inevitably, weaker in the shank. Last, sharpen the hook yourself.

Some skippers prefer to bait up for you. If you've no experience, then allow this. However, I feel this dampens the enjoyment of a successful capture. There's a hint more fun when you've baited up, struck, hooked, and played your own fish. This interference goes even further when skippers pick up the rod and strike the fish for you. This is not fishing and you're wrong if you think it is.

The night before a prospective trip, I like to telephone the skipper to check that all is well. The skipper can advise you on weather problems and, more importantly, give you an update on how the previous few days have gone regarding shark catches. If the weather is not good and the skipper won't sail, respect his judgement – it matters little that media weather reports beg to differ. Skippers are at sea for much of their lives; they learn to read the signs of forthcoming storms and squalls. On the other hand, some unscrupulous skippers use this dodge to save face when they've double booked. One or two may try to add a couple of extra people to a fully paid-up group of only three or four. Stand your ground on this: if you've paid full money for the boat with only three or four people stipulated to fish, then that is how it must be.

When a big fish is caught, pay attention to the fact that the skipper played an important part. Too many reports give only the details of the captor and the fight – give credit where it's due and your relationship with the boat and its owner will become lasting and more profitable for you both. Finally, if there are hot drinks on board still take your own cup. Too many times there are four cups and six people on board – a small point, but a valid one.

Top-class boats have all the above facilities, especially in the US where services are first class. Most British shark boats are reasonably well equipped but not up to the standards of the American ones. Perhaps when catches increase and the band of shark fishers grows, British boats will also work to higher standards as they cater for the increased demand.

PRIVATE BOATS

When you hire a professional boat, you eliminate much of the work that falls on a private boat-owner. Many feel that it's less of an achievement to catch a large shark on a professional boat than it is to capture a smaller shark on your own vessel. Logically, this is the case. Hiring skippers also gives you access to their knowledge of the shark's whereabouts, their skill in handling the boat when the engines are needed to regain lost line, and their experience in tailing the fish when beaten. Private boat-owners take all this upon their own heads, as well as the responsibilities for crew safety, etc.

However, more and more people now own their own boats and, as a consequence, I foresee a rapid growth in small-boat shark-fishing, particularly in the waters around the British coast. American anglers have a head start, but there is still room for growth.

BOAT DESIGN

The modern concept of fast, planing hulls pushed along by huge outboard motors worries me – this type of boat relies on the surface water being relatively calm. It is ideal for pushing out a long way in calm weather to fish marks otherwise out of bounds to slower craft. Many owners of such fast boats claim the speed of which their craft are capable is their prime safety asset; they feel their speed will get them home more quickly when bad weather threatens.

This argument has some basis when incoming bad weather can be timed and forecast very accurately – an unlikely occurrence in my experience. With more than ten years' experience on such craft, I rarely find that ideal conditions at the beginning of the trip still persist on the return. What invariably happens is that a breeze comes with the turn of the tide, and the flat seas of the morning gain a short chop or begin to lift in an uneasy swell. Your advantage of speed is immediately much reduced.

When this weather change happens quickly and without warning (and you're far away from your home port) you realize the inadequacy of such hulls. To gain speed these hulls sacrifice stability; the bow slams hard against oncoming waves instead of cutting through them. This is because the hull sits on top of the water as opposed to in it.

In bad conditions, these hulls drift from side to side under low power. They are designed to steer at high speed not slow revs. When you need to quarter a rising swell, the planing hull is pushed and lifted until the boat is beam on. This is hard work for the person at the helm, who tries to manoeuvre the boat back to its true course. It creates a very uncomfortable and sometimes frightening return trip for the other occupants.

The main advantage of the flat, planing hull is that, in calmish weather, they are stable and offer huge amounts of working space for a relatively small boat. In ideal conditions some hulls travel at speeds in excess of 37km/h (20kn) with the appropriate motor. For use as a shark boat, some designs have too little freeboard or depth of gunnel. When a person leans over one side to tail a fish, this can bring the water level dangerously high up the side of the boat. Short grab-rails are a good safety feature. These can be made so that they lift out when necessary for tailing or releasing fish. Such a boat needs a small cuddy, or short cabin, in which you can protect your equipment, especially any electronics you need to carry, and yourselves. This keeps the rear of the boat, or cockpit area, free of clutter for the fighting of fish.

The smallest length of boat I would use to venture more than a mile or two offshore would be 5m (16ft). These offer reasonable sea-keeping qualities and a good degree of safety. In the company of other boats, and by carrying a VHF radio and proper compass, you could work ground as far out as 10 miles (16km) or more in ideal conditions. Such a boat also has the advantage of being easily towed for freedom of movement. However, I feel more at ease with a length of 6m (18ft). The extra length and beam creates more stability for working offshore. Having two, medium, outboard motors working in conjunction with each other is acceptable, as both of them breaking down at the same time is unlikely. However, I prefer one, large, power unit for speed and a smaller unit for trolling and emergencies.

Semi-displacement hulls are an attempt to compromise between keeping a good top speed and maintaining stability. In practice they fail to achieve either: I don't like these hulls and would not consider owning one for small-boat sharking. A full displacement hull does as its name

suggests – it is designed as a rounded V-shape sitting in the water as opposed to on it, as the planing hull does. The displacement hull displaces its own mass in water. These hulls are stable when underway, and the sharp bow cuts through oncoming waves. They are, however, much slower. Speeds of only 11–15km/h (6–8kn) can be expected as an average, which therefore limits their operating range when time is short or when the shark grounds lie well offshore. On the other hand, they offer vastly superior sea-keeping qualities. This gives them a far greater safety value when you are caught in deteriorating weather. When at anchor, displacement hulls tend to roll a little as you would expect and, in the smaller boats, space inside is limited.

With all this in mind, if I was limited to a length of 5m (16ft) I would rather go fishing in a planing hull than a displacement hull of the same size. For inshore work, say up to 8 miles (13km) out, 6m (18ft) would be my target length, with a beam of 2m (7ft) or more. In this size of boat I would opt for an inboard diesel engine as opposed to an outboard. My ideal boat for private shark-fishing would be a displacement hull of fibreglass construction some 6.5m by 2.4m (21ft by 8ft) in size, with a wheelhouse up front to protect the equipment, electronics, and the crew. An inboard diesel engine is both reliable and economical, and you have easy access for electricity to run the sounder, radio, etc. A boat of this size is able to tackle pretty well any shark and provides an ideal platform to fight it. A craft of this size is, of course, too big to tow easily behind a car but, in my opinion, it is the safest boat for private usage.

With the proper equipment aboard, a working range in good weather could exceed 20 miles (30km). Even if a sudden, unpredicted gale came out of nowhere, I would have full confidence in such a boat making its way to safety without major problems.

Very small porbeagle pups can be brought onto the boat for careful unhooking. To do this, all tackle and equipment must be stowed and the shark's tail held up against the gunnel to restrict its movement. Fish over 34 kg (75 lb) should not be lifted onto the boat until well and truly dead. Big problems occur with sharks over 45 kg (100 lb) caught from a small boat and which you wish to take back to port. A system I've used with some success, and that I find adequate for fish of a reasonable size is as follows (I've yet to have the opportunity of trying it on a real monster but feel confident in it when the time arrives). Gaffs are out of place on small boats; tailing the shark is the only method advised. I use a strong rope tailer for this. The length of rope should be about 3m (10ft) long, which includes a large sliding loop at one end and a small tied-in loop at the other. The sliding loop is tightened around the shark's tail. The small loop is for the attachment of large floats. I use 23-l (5-gal) plastic jerry cans. These are bound crossways with rope, leaving a short length at either end. To one end I attach a climber's snap-link karabiner and form a loop in the other. The karabiner is clipped onto the small tailer loop, and the spare loop on the can will take a second karabiner to connect a second can. If necessary, the cans can be released and allowed to float away from the boat. No sharks can take the cans below the surface and they will drown.

Alternatively, a long rope can be attached to the spare loop on the second container. This rope is then fastened to a cleat or sampson post on the stern. The sharks can then be towed backwards until drowned. This method is simple and quick. The tailer will not come undone from the shark's tail once tightened. Be very careful of the stress you impose on some modern

boats through the cleats – I've seen these torn out completely. If you need to set up two lines, attach one to each cleat to spread the load. The beauty of this container system is that it minimizes the time a shark is held at the side of the boat. Some boats may not take kindly to being thumped by the tail of a powerful shark.

Small boats can be used very successfully with big fish. The boat's extra drag when released from the anchor and allowed to drift helps tire the shark. I once played a fish that pulled the stern of an 11-m (36-ft) steel boat round into the tide, and this on just 8-kg (18-lb) line. In fact, when hooking a shark from a small boat, I'd always suggest retrieving the anchor and letting the fish tow the boat.

With a boat of less than 6m (21ft), I wouldn't fish more than two people. With three on board, space is at a premium. On occasions a third pair of hands would be useful, but a well-practised twosome can handle pretty well any situation. It goes without saying that both parties should be well versed in handling the boat, as well as radio and safety procedures.

Certain aspects of etiquette should be observed when at sea and in the presence of other shark boats. Never cross the chum trail of a drifting or anchored boat. When necessary, do so by waiting until a distance of several hundred metres has elapsed or, better still, motor well uptide and cross the boat's bows. I've seen boats actually anchor inside another boat's chum trail. This is bad manners and must be avoided. Never anchor close to another boat: leave at least a couple of hundred metres and preferably more. There's no benefit in trying to poach fish from another boat's slick. It's far better to make sure that your dubby is fresh and gives the shark the stronger scent to follow.

Priority should be given to a boat that is playing a shark. This is one reason I prefer to see boats in the same area spread well apart. A running shark can easily find another boat's anchor rope or anglers' lines. This is an expensive loss for both boats.

I like to keep radio chatter to a polite minimum. Never tell another craft that you have shark around the boat; if they try to take advantage of the situation, their motors and general noise can actually attract the sharks towards them.

SEASICKNESS

I have included a few words on seasickness because, contrary to popular belief, no person is totally immune. The worst thing you can do is to drink alcohol the night before a trip. Your body takes well over 24 hours to recover from the effects of drink, and this can affect not only your stomach but also, and more importantly, your balance. Avoid greasy foods the day before a trip. Prior to setting sail, eat a sensible breakfast — ideally, lightly but-tered toast and cereal with skimmed milk.

Food on board needs to be eaten on the basis of a little and often. A good choice would be chicken or non-fatty red meat. Tomatoes and celery can be eaten in the hand and are refreshing. Apples are good and help to quench a thirst. Dry biscuits with no fat content can help ease an other-wise volatile stomach.

By all means use a proprietary brand of seasickness pills. If nothing else, they do give a psychological boost. Some pills can cause drowsiness, so try several brands until you find one that suits you. The best I've ever come across goes by the name of Stugeron. Try to stay busy. Keep watching the balloons and talking to other anglers. If you feel really ill, watch the horizon. This can help to restore your balance. Avoid the smell of cooking food and the engine's diesel-fuel fumes. Anch-ored up at night with no visual horizon can be the worst situation for inducing

seasickness. You can only follow the suggestions above and hope for the best. It's surprising how someone who says they are about to die from seasickness suddenly comes alive when the ratchet on the shark reel sounds. It's the best cure I know. Always carry a flannel dampened in fresh water and sealed in a plastic bag. A quick wipe over the face freshens you up no end.

CLOTHING

Always carry a hat — too much sun will create not only sore skin but also in extreme cases hallucinations. This is not funny; I've seen several people suffer and have been close to it myself. A good barrier-cream also helps the skin avoid the worst of the sun's ulra-violet light as it reflects off the sea. Sunglasses not only shield you from the sun, they also help you see deeper into the water on very bright days.

Shoes are the most important item. Proper yachting shoes afford good grip, both when moving about or when playing a fish. Short, rubber Wellingtons are only acceptable when the trip is aboard a boat with open scuppers, or it's raining. Shirts should have open necks and be made of a cool substance such as cotton. For warmth, several light, thin jumpers are far better than a single thick one.

Wet-weather gear should be of top quality. I prefer a bib-and-brace type that keeps the worst of the dubby and blood off you, and you can wash it down with the ship's hose. Jackets should have a hood and allow plenty of room for movement around the shoulders. Some jackets pull tight under the arms when the arms are outstretched, which causes discomfort when fighting a fish; and that isn't funny either, over several hours of strenuous engagement.

SUNDRIES

I also carry a good pair of binoculars. These are useful for looking to the distant edge of the chum trail and for picking up shark fins on the surface as they cruise towards you. Cameras need careful looking after. A plastic bucket with a sealable lid in a bright, easily recognizable colour houses my cameras. These are protected from knocks and bangs by a cushion of thick foam hollowed out in the middle. The trouble is that, with only two on the boat, you rarely get time to use them. I always carry a sharp knife in a small belt-pouch. This is rarely used but has occasionally been needed in an emergency. The scope of this book does not allow for a full inventory of boat safety equipment. It is enough to suggest that only fools would venture to sea without life-jackets, spare anchor and rope, flares, fuel, and a working radio. Always leave your expected return time with a reliable person on shore, and give them a rough idea of the area you will be working.

CHAPTER 13

Shore Fishing

Back in the early 1960s, a remarkable Irish angler, Jack Shine, proved possible what many thought to be impossible. Mr Shine set out deliberately to catch shark from the shore and succeeded with several big fish of up to 62 kg (138 lb). These fish came from Green Island at the mouth of Liscannor Bay. As far as I can ascertain, these are the only shark to have been taken from the British Isles from the shore.

Many varieties of shark can be taken from relatively shallow water in other parts of the world. I spent several years working in Australia and found small sand sharks, duskies, wobbegongs, and others a frequent capture on ledgered fish baits. Successfully capturing these fish on a regular basis was only possible when you knew that your quarry was in the vicinity – you were more prepared to put the necessary time in, thus increasing your chances of success.

Very few anglers have the determination to persist in the search for shore shark. Blank months and even seasons can be expected. Boredom from lack of action will quickly defeat all but a minute minority. Having said this, porbeagles are the ideal target for shore success, as Jack Shine proved. They frequently come very close in. The British record fish was hooked only 180m (200yd) from shore. These sharks often swim in water with a depth of only 6m (20ft).

Forget beach work – concentrate on rock marks that give into deep water. British shores and perhaps parts of Europe hold the very best opportunities. In Britain, the coast of Devon and Cornwall is, for the most part, formed of steep cliffs that fall sheer to the sea and hold a good depth of water close in, particularly the area around Hartland Point and down to Newquay. This is where most boat sharking is done, which proves the fish are there and feeding, and this encourages persistence.

The coast of mid-Wales from St David's to Newquay also looks favourable, consisting of cliffs with deep water at their base. The Lleyn Peninsula and parts of Anglesey in North Wales, along with much of the west and northern coast of Scotland, also falls into this category. If I had the opportunity for a prolonged search, it would be at the south-west tip of Ireland: from Ross Carbery, following the coast right around past Baltimore as far as the mouth of the Shannon and beyond, the inshore ground is ideal for encouraging porbeagles right in under the cliffs.

The area between Castlehaven and Baltimore is, for the most part, bounded by cliffs. On trips here to look into the ground-fishing potential, and to fish for blue shark, I've seen fins within 275m (300yd) of the shore. Many of the rock marks in this area have more than 10m (30ft) of water directly below the cliff's base. The food supply is outstanding, with quantities of pollack and mackerel.

The ideal shore mark would not only need depth and hold good stocks of food but would also need to have a tide-run. How else will you get the balloon and bait, and extend the chum trail, away from the shore? You must take care of your safety and your ease in actually gaffing a fish and retrieving it across and up the rocks. The best marks are usually found where a tidal run hugs the coast and is then forced out by a projecting finger of rock. A balloon worked from here will travel a long way. Such a projection also creates rough water, encouraging shoals of pollack and mackerel to take up residence.

Pay attention to the admiralty charts of the area to see if there are any major rock uplifts in the deeper water a shark could swim around and break the line. This also applies to the inshore surface. Lobster-pot buoys should be noted and allowed for. A close survey of the immediate area, in an arc of 450m (500yd), should be undertaken until a map of the under-sea area forms in your mind. The tidal influence on any inshore sharks is more likely to affect ease of food availability than actual tidal size. Having said that, I would avoid the smaller neaps and the very biggest spring tides, concentrating on the more usual feeding tides of average height and run.

A hunch of mine is that porbeagles may visit inshore areas only when offshore food supplies are poor. A careful check on how the boat anglers are doing for mackerel may give you a clue as to where the sharks may be. A stable food supply of small pollack near the cliffs would be very appealing to a hungry shark. Also, a peak of feeding activity occurs around dusk and it could be then (and at dawn) that the greatest chance of a run will come. A chum trail worked all night could perhaps pay better dividends than a daytime attempt.

The peak times for porbeagle to be close inshore are likely to be April and May when mackerel are in short supply and the sharks are looking to pollack and coalfish to fill the gap. I would anticipate a lull during June and July, with a fresh influx during August and September before we lose the porbeagles to deeper waters. This early-autumn period coincides with the peak numbers of mackerel inshore.

Using chum as in boat fishing is a problem. Unless you have the good fortune to locate a run of tide that leaves your feet, and heads out to deep water, the flow of chum will be a restricted one. I can't see many anglers actually carrying ready-made chum with them — many of these marks will require a long walk across rough country to reach them. I prefer to take a quantity of bran that, unmixed, is very light, and a small bottle of pilchard oil. I feather mackerel (which are usually about in sufficient numbers at such places) and create two bags of mix. One is the bran and oil mixed with mackerel. I fillet the mackerel, crushing the fillets in my hands. This is put into a fine-weave onion sack that stops the flow of scent washing out too quickly. The heads and bodies of the mackerel are simply put together in a sack to add blood to the water. Both bags are suspended from ropes that can be shortened to allow for the rise of the tide. The finer mix can have a quantity of emulsifier added to aid dispersal. This should be placed where a current offsets against the face of a cliff or rocky edge.

A few small pieces of chopped mackerel can be added to fall to the seabed or drift with the current to bring any deep-lurking shark upwards. I also try to take advantage of an ebbing tide that takes the smell out into deeper water offshore. This covers more ground and should bring fish in towards you.

You need a float that catches any offshore wind – again to gain distance. Several types of floats have been tried, including one that incorporated a plastic sail. However none of them impressed me; they all need complicated release systems when a shark seizes a bait and so become unreliable. I've used a kite made from plastic sheet with a large, split clip to hold the reel line. Again, this is unreliable. Not being much of a kite flyer, I found the kite would spiral down and around when the wind eased or backed, fouling the following reel line. The resulting tangle needs to be retrieved to be sorted out, and this wastes too much time. I still use a slightly over-inflated balloon. This is pushed along quite adequately by a favourable breeze. At times, a float is a nuisance, preventing the bait from following a weak tidal current when the wind so dictates. If this is the case, use a small plastic bottle partially filled with water. This sits lower in the water, catching less of the wind. Remember, a float is not needed for visual bite registration – its only function is to suspend the bait and wire trace at a predetermined depth.

I always use a free-running swivel on the main line, with weak line to hold the balloon. This compensates for the balloon spinning with the tide – something more prone to happen close to shore because of the rapid change of tidal currents. Close inshore, porbeagles tend to swim nearer to the surface so I rarely set my baits deeper than 7.5m (25ft). This also avoids the worst of the smaller bottom fish looking for an easy meal. Use one-third of the total depth available as a starting guide.

Tackle, as already mentioned, should be kept as simple as possible. Traces are 1–1.2-m (3–4-ft) lengths of standard wire direct to the hook, but the normal, heavy-duty mono trace is replaced by a 1.5-m (5-ft) section of 90-kg (200-lb) wire. I consider this necessary as any shark hooked

and brought to the base of the cliff is likely to snag the trace on the rocks and the mono would be too weak a link. Traces longer than this are unmanageable for practical fishing.

I also choose a smaller hook (usually an 8/0 Sea Demon) that will sink into the jaw better on relatively light tackle. This should be inserted in the bait as normal but left well clear of the flesh for the point to engage the shark's jaw easily. The general size of bait is, usually, smaller. A 4-m (12-ft) beach rod of strong construction is my first choice, coupled with a 4/0-sized lever drag or equivalant star-drag reel. This gives a slightly unbalanced unit, but little other tackle has the pedigree and line capacity needed. Besides, casting is not possible with this type of gear.

Fill the reel with line of between 9 and 11 kg (20 and 25 lb). This may seem light, but you will be fighting the shark with a pressure of only a kilogram or so exerted by the rod. It's the amount of line available that will land you your fish, not the line strength.

Any porbeagles hooked close to shore will run like fury. This will be more so when the shark is hooked only a few metres from solid rock and in relatively shallow water. My own experience abroad suggests that you always let the shark run as far as it wants, only applying pressure when it slows. Any effort on your part to try to turn a fish away from a snag will inevitably result in failure. The tackle in use, and the distance between you and the shark, negates any such action.

Shore fishing is one of only two situations in which I would recommend using a gaff (see p 73). This needs to be both long and very strong. A several-sectioned handle, either home-made, constructed from chimney-sweepers rods or drainage rods, is fine, but the section should be pinned in some way to avoid any tendency to twist open. The gaff should also be tied to a strong rope of sufficient thickness to offer some grip when held. An iron rod hammered into the rock is a better anchorage than a lump of rock. The angler who goes down to gaff the shark should also be fixed to the same iron peg by a stout rope – for safety's sake.

Once gaffed, the fish should be dragged out of the water and stunned with heavy blows administered in the vicinity of the eyes. A second rope around the tail would then secure the fish. This is a two-person operation whenever possible, for safety reasons. So few people in Britain have tried for shore sharks that little is really known of their frequency close to shore. For a few very keen, single-minded and determined anglers, willing to learn from their mistakes, the reward of a first shore shark is the ultimate achievement. One shark from the shore is worth a hundred from boats.

CHAPTER 14

Tackle

RODS

Virtually all fishing-rod manufacturers claim that one or two of their range are suitable for shark-fishing. For the most part, these rods are a compromise, failing to fulfil the exacting standards an experienced shark fisher requires. The modern idea of a short butt married to a long-tip, two-piece rod is a good one. The two pieces are joined by a male-into-female spigot system. This should be held solid by a screw-threaded alloy nut. The nut is usually part of the tip section and mates to threads on the female butt.

The butt section should be constructed from aircraft-grade alloy for lightness and strength. The fibreglass tip may have a mix of carbon in it to add strength, again without adding weight. This can cause problems, although this should be rare with a recognized brand. Too much carbon content in a blank can cause a rod to shatter without warning when under pressure: I've seen this happen too many times.

Pure fibreglass rods with no carbon content are smooth and bend fully when under load. Their strength is increased by an extra thickness of material, which destroys any weight advantage. A standard form of glassfibre is E glass; S glass is an uprated version, being stronger and lighter. Plain fibreglass rods have less feel and go sloppy when under full power. Adding carbon to the mix stiffens the rod,

makes it lighter, and adds more feel to the fish's fight. A rod of this type is the one I'd put my trust in.

A blank's actual action needs careful understanding. An all-through, action rod that bends to the butt under full load is said to protect the line from sudden overload. This is, to some extent, true. However, when big fish need to be lifted off the bottom or pumped back to the boat from a distance, their lack of backbone often defeats the angler. Fast taper rods that have a forgiving movement in the upper tip section with stiff (in fact, very stiff) mid-sections are favoured by many top anglers. They prefer these rods for lifting fish when a given blank's ultimate power is required.

I opt for a middle-of-the-road blank. Some tip action with a little give in the mid-section allows for feel during the fight, and the angler is kept better informed as to how much pressure is being applied. I also believe that the gentle give in the blank helps tire fish better than the dead, solid pull of the stiffer rods. Ideally, the lower tip section and butt should give a little, then lock solid for lifting big fish. Modern compositions of fibreglass, with carbon or graphite content, are a good blend for this form of rod, together with suitable designs and wall thicknesses.

A rod's power is found by measuring the weight it requires to pull the tip over at a right angle to the butt – in other words, a quarter circle. This is known as the test curve, and the rod imposes maximum power in that position. To gauge line strength suitable for a given rod, it is necessary to increase fivefold the actual weight needed to pull a blank into that quarter circle. For example, a rod needing 1 kg (2 lb) of weight to reach its test curve could safely be used, as a general rule, with lines of 5 kg (10 lb). If 2 kg (4 lb) of weight was needed, allow lines to 10 kg (20 lb). A 3-kg (6-lb) weight gives the opportunity for lines of 14 kg (30 lb) to be used, and so on. In reality, you have about a 25-per-cent leeway either side, although properly balanced tackle is always best.

Today, most boat rods are sold on a line-class system based on the formulae just described. A 20-lb-class rod is suitable for 20-lb line, 30-lb-class for 30-lb line, and so on. Rods are bought worldwide by the pound-class system; kilos are rarely quoted. However, in Britain rods of 30-lb class are equivalent to an American 20. Supposedly, this is because British waters have few big-game fish that tax tackle to the limit. I don't agree! Although the billfishes, and so on, are absent from British shores (at least, the experts say they are) a porbeagle of 136 or 180 kg (300 or 400 lb) fights every bit as hard as shark of similar size elsewhere. When using perfectly balanced tackle like this, I prefer to use line a kilogram or so lighter than the test curve suggests, for example, 8-kg (18-lb) line with a 20-class rod. This matters most if you are keen on line-class records, where the line must part below the strength of the tackle being used. Stiffer rod actions suit mono lines better, while users of braided lines prefer softer actions. This is because mono stretches and braided lines do not.

The average rod length set by manufacturers persists at around 2m (7ft). Some, more forward-thinking makers, offer slightly longer rods: 2m (7ft) is the absol-

ute minimum for a boat rod, but 2.5m (8ft) would be better. This gives more control when a fish is brought to the side of the boat and exacts more leverage against a fish during play. The rod's action can also be better balanced than that evident in a shorter version.

Rod fittings should be chosen first for strength and, second, for lightness. Roller tips are useful as they help cut down on line friction, making the retrieval of line under pressure a little easier; however, these are not essential. This applies less than one might think when you consider that the line is only retrieved when rod pressure is minimal. In line classes of up to 50 class, roller tips are not strictly necessary. You certainly don't need a full set on a rod. The extra weight cancels out any advantage. The best roller tips I've used are AFTCOs. These are solidly constructed and perform well under all trials. Other makes may be equally as good but should be judged against AFTCOs. Standard, bridge-type rings are adequate as intermediates, and they have the advantage of bending a little more with the rod than do the full roller type.

Rod hand-grips must offer non-slip grip when wet and be long enough to accommodate the full width of your hand – plus a little more. Modern foam materials make the best grips and are unaffected by persistent submersion in saltwater. They are prone to damage by sharp objects, etc., but are easy to replace.

Reel seats these days are invariably made from plastics or a carbon-fibre mix. These are fine, provided you use the reel clamp that comes with your reel for extra stability. Check that the reel-seat lugs sit snugly inside the rod's reel seat – many don't! This causes excessive wear and the reel may wobble from side to side when line is wound back. Some reel seats are simply glued to the alloy butt. This is permissible if done properly. It entails roughing up the section of the butt where the seat will fit, and applying plenty of slow-setting glue. Two-part epoxy glues are the strongest, yet they will flex a little when needed. The seat should be pushed and at the same time twisted in a clockwise motion up the butt and into the correct position. Excess glue should be kept away from the screw threads. I always protect all the outer reel-seat surface and upper part of the butt with masking-tape. This is easily removed when the job is done.

Where the rod tip is aligned to the butt with locating lugs, make sure the reel-seat lugs line up with the rings on the tip before leaving a freshly glued seat. Occasional re-alignment may be needed until the glue begins to cure. Grips below the reel seat are unnecessary, yet many manufacturers insist on using them, probably for appearance. Plain shrink tube is more practical as it protects the alloy tube by sealing out saltwater and is easy to keep clean.

Butt caps are essential to avoid accidents, but many rods come with a gimbal slot hidden by the cap. I dislike such gimbal systems that link with a pin in the cap off a butt pad worn around the angler's middle.

Some superb blanks come with either slightly inferior fittings or they need some modification to suit the owner better. The workmanship can also be shoddy – reel seats work loose and whippings on rings are poorly protected. Experience of such things means that I now always build my own rods from scratch: in this way I know the job has been done properly. All ring feet should be gently tapered at the points so that the whipping thread rides neatly up them. Also, I check that both feet sit flat on the blank. I avoid any feet that lift towards the point. Relying on the thread to compensate results in excessive pressure being placed on the whippings.

I under-whip all ring feet, using fine thread – usually Gudebrod size A. I

measure the full width of both ring feet as a total and allow 1cm ($\frac{1}{2}$in) either side. The under-whipping covers the full length. This is sealed using several thin coats of a modern epoxy coating, but only fill until the turns of the thread disappear. This must now be allowed to dry fully. The rings are now whipped on over this, using a thicker thread, Gudebrod size D, leaving the under-whipping showing for $\frac{1}{2}$cm ($\frac{1}{4}$in) at both ends. The main whipping should have six good coatings of finish, with a gentle rub down after the third and fifth coats. This gives a mirror finish when done properly and it's the strongest fixing a ring can have. I work in the darker colours of thread as this gives a slightly better finish and the turns of thread are invisible when completed.

Some roller-tip rings are too loose when slid over the tip of a blank, and are too loose to be glued. If this is the case, a thin under-whipping of either A-size thread or, if you need something even thinner, a de-stranded section of A thread, is now built up along the length of the tip where the roller will fit – just until the roller tube slides over easily. I use hot-melt glue for all tip rings as this is easily removed when the time comes for a replacement. I'm told that hot-melt glue can move when temperatures exceed 30°C (86°F), but I have never experienced any problems with this. Force plenty of the glue down the ring tube, which should be warmed until the glue melts. Quickly place this over the tip and align the ring with the intermediate rings. Any excess that oozes out almost guarantees a good joint. This can be easily removed when it has gone hard with your fingernail. A small length of whipping below the tip ring tube finishes the rod off.

I hate to see a rod carelessly leant against the stern, where all manner of damage from knocks and chaffing can befall it. To keep the worst buffeting at bay, place a short length of foam tube, split on one side, over the rod. This cushions it and stops it rolling about, yet does not interfere with the line flow when a shark runs.

At the very end of every trip, your rods should be washed in warm water to which a little washing-up detergent has been added. A fine toothbrush gets grime out from around the rod rings. When the rod has well and truly dried, I apply a coat of turtle wax, preferably the liquid sort as opposed to gel. This simple procedure avoids major salt penetration. It pays to carry all rods in a length of plastic tube. Total care of the rod means there will be no broken rings or worse damage that may not be noticed until you are far out to sea.

REELS

Considering the advances made in shore-fishing reels and the lighter end of the boat market, little that's new and note-worthy has happened to the game reels from a 4/0 size upwards. A few firms have introduced new models but reports of poor replacement of parts and service have put regular anglers on their guard. Much depends on the quick replacement of broken or worn parts and also on their availability; trips and fish can be lost because of delayed replacement parts. Always carry a few of the items most likely to let you down. Anti-reverse dogs wear as do clutch washers. A couple of spare side-plate screws may also come in handy.

Many of the reels currently available have been on the market for many years: Fin Nor, Hardys, Everols, and, of course, Penn, are all quality lever drags with an impressive pedigree. They are well made and have a good service back-up. The Penns are the most frequently seen and are superb reels without being overly expensive.

The lever-drag system can be finely set to give line under very fine pressure – a valuable asset when fishing balanced tackle. Also, the greater area of brake disc in proportion to the star-drag clutch offers less likelihood of the disc overheating when a big fish takes a prolonged run. Star drags should not be ignored. If properly maintained and used correctly they are almost the equal of the lever drag. However, star drags suffer from heating up when a large fish runs for several hundred metres. The clutch may also grab at times, which will part the line, although this is usually due to bad maintenance. Penn Senators (from an older generation) and other makes once employed asbestos washers to avoid the worst of this heating-up problem. These can be improved by coating the washers with graphite powder. This smooths the clutch and it is a superb lubricant, avoiding the grab effect.

As Senators are still the most-used star-drag reels, being available from the small 1/0 size right up to the massive 16/0, it's worth mentioning that Penn manufacture a conversion kit to replace the old asbestos washers in the older Penns. This wonderful modern material (HT100) gives a smooth and reliable clutch that is not prone to locking up. Most reels from a 4/0 size up will have harness lugs as standard. Bigger reels, such as 9/0s, will have rod braces that tighten the reel onto the rod as extra insurance against sideways movement.

Big reels are sometimes provided with a choice of alloy or brass spools. Alloy spools might collapse under the pressure of tightening mono line. Where possible, always opt for the solid-brass spool. Although it adds extra weight to the reel, it is far stronger and will not collapse. Forged-alloy spools used in the top-quality range of reels are superb, being both light-weight and of high strength.

Fast gearing on a shark reel is not as desirable as it may first appear. The angler may be retrieving line as a fish comes to life and suddenly changes direction. The sudden strain imposed by the shark swimming one way and the line being reeled in another causes the line to snap tight. Even strong line cannot withstand this instant pressure. Slower gears help to avoid this. Because of the necessary fine cut needed to engineer these fast gears, they are also weaker than slower gears and less able to withstand heavy pressure. Under extreme load they may actually strip.

Do-it-yourself maintenance of your reels is essential. You may have to strip a reel completely during a trip at some stage. Sending reels back to the maker for service or to a repair shop is costly, both in time and money.

Using oil — even thick oil — is not the best lubricant for spool spindles and gear stems. I use thick machine grease that protects the moving parts and adds a hint of braking to the spool. Any bearings are soaked in warmed oil of at least 90 grade. Don't be heavy handed with lubricants or they spread everywhere and attract dirt. Spools are stripped of line and given a coat of wax polish before re-loading. The layer of polish helps to avoid corrosion by saltwater imprisoned on the line. The outside of the reels are rinsed in warm water and then scrubbed with a toothbrush, allowed to dry, and given a coat of wax polish to ward off salt deposits. Only lightly oil, with pilchard oil, handles and reel studs for bracket attachment. This avoids the transmission of foreign smells from your hands either into the dubby or onto the hook bait.

Some manufacturers make reels compatible with 12- and 20-class rods. These are excellent and perform well. However, some star drags and new lever drags are equally good and much cheaper. ABU used to market lever drags in the 20 and 30 classes but have ceased to do so, which is a shame. However, their 10,000c is excellent. Many of my 9-kg (20-lb) class porbeagles have come on this reel. The drag, although a star, is precise and avoids locking-up problems. I do, though, take the precaution of replacing the drag washers with new ones after every long fight or prolonged trip.

Penn have brought out a light-weight 4/0 lever drag with carbon side-plates. Again, this has the capacity for light-line work and, being backed up by Penn's usual reliability, should be a good choice. The Daiwa lever drag LD50 is excellent — it is fine and precise, and the line capacity of 8 kg (18 lb) is just about right. All these models are available virtually worldwide.

Smaller reels need more precise maintenance. Grease (lightly applied to the main gear stem) protects the gears' centres as they revolve. In warm weather, the grease also remains solid. Ordinary oils become thin and runny during warm weather, leaving the gear stem and gears virtually dry. This causes excessive wear under load. Use the same grease to lubricate the gear teeth.

The spool spindles may be either an integral part of the spool or the spool may revolve freely on a static spindle. In either case, I use a thickish motor oil, say a minimum of 20/50, or more likely straight 30 grade. Always go for 30 when conditions and temperatures are hot. A star-drag reel needs the drag washers to be freely coated in graphite grease. Some anglers use candle wax but this is not a good choice. If a fish runs hard and long the wax can melt causing high and low spots on the washers. This comes out as a grab-and-release drag.

Line needs to be loaded with care. Lay the line in tight, touching turns, cotton-reel fashion. I load all my reels until they won't take any more line — right up to the spool's lip. Even though you apply a constant pressure to the line when you first load it, it will sit tighter on the spool when you're fishing and retrieving. Use the spool knot to attach the reel line to the spool as described in the section on knots later in this chapter.

Small reels benefit from having a protective strip of insulation-tape fitted over each side-plate and the gap where the cage touches the side-plate. This guards the side-plate from scratches and keeps excess water out. All reel spools should be set so that a little side-play is noted. This avoids wear on the spindle ends.

Reel handles should be soused frequently in a solvent to remove any persistent deposits of dirt, but be careful – some solvents may eat into the plastic handle and only oil with pilchard oil. Pay particular attention to any wear on the ratchet tooth and anti-reverse dog. These are often the first to complain on lighter reels. Keep any lubricant on these light and to a minimum. Thick grease or the like can stop movement of the anti-reverse dog. I use none on the reverse dog and so have to accept frequent replacements of the tooth.

Ball-bearings help smooth the retrieval of line. These should be lubricated with a medium-weight oil of 30 grade, but on big 9/0 reels and above go for 90 grade. Fill a tablespoon with some of the oil and heat this over a stove. When the oil has thinned, the clean and dry bearing is placed in the oil, which should completely cover the bearing. Little bubbles of air will be emitted from the bearing as the oil soaks in. When these bubbles cease, the carriage is full of oil. No other system gets oil to the heart of the bearing.

The inside edges of spools and side-plates can be protected with WD40. I prefer one of the modern sprays that sets to a very clear, rubbery coating. Apply this sparingly to the plain surfaces, keeping it away from any moving parts.

After use, all reels should be rinsed in warm water and left to dry in a warm atmosphere – either in an airing-cupboard or slightly away from a radiator or heater, but not too close or the side-plates on some reels may warp. Always transport your reels in a proper reel bag. This prevents unnecessary scratches and other damage to both reel and line that may lose you fish in the future.

When choosing a reel (especially for lighter-line fishing) it can be prudent to select a model a size larger than needed. This offers the advantages of a drag system and gears that are well on top of the job required and, more importantly, the reel has a greater spool capacity. Many top-rank anglers do this as a matter of course.

Any light-line reel needs a line capacity exceeding 450m (500yd) – 640m (700yd) being a better margin of safety. Again, remember that as a spool empties of line the drag increases proportionately. It's up to the angler to pay constant attention to this and ease the drag when a big fish runs a long way from the boat.

LINE

Line choice is between ordinary monofilament or braided line. Braided lines are built from an interweaving of individual strands of material into a single line, the material usually being Terylene. A woven line is heavier than mono and has a greater overall diameter for a given strength than mono. It also stretches far less than mono. This has the advantage in bite detection but only when the rod is held, which is rare in shark-fishing. Also, when the line is loaded under heavy pressure, it exerts less force on the spool than mono. A base of 90m (100yd) of braided line before the mono can soak up any pressure the tightening mono may exert.

Polyester has been tried in the construction of braided lines and offers a finer diameter in relation to breaking strain than the standard Terylene product. However, I find braided line far less durable than mono. It will not stand any minor surface abrasions. These abrasions continue to de-strand under load, whereas mono will take a high degree of surface damage and still not part. Neither is a braided line immune from sunlight and its weakening effect. It has a higher resistance factor than mono but will lose up to 60 per cent of its strength after persistent exposure.

Braided lines can be a good choice for trolling as, being heavier, they help work the line deeper and, having less stretch, they aid the setting of the hook. The biggest disadvantage is that of the increase in diameter causing water friction to a taking shark. Porbeagles are more inclined to drop a bait fished on a braided line after a short run. I'm sure this is because of the excessive drag. I now never use braided lines for all these reasons, and also because mono is far cheaper and therefore allows frequent changes.

To recognize good-quality nylon line, you need to appreciate the defects apparent in a bad line. Cost (or lack of it) creates the initial suspicions. Our fears are further heightened when we note bad colouring, a high rate of twisting and kinking, a large diameter for a relatively low breaking strain, poor knot strength and closure (either grossly stiff or extremely limp), a shape and size that varies throughout the length, and an exaggerated or non-existent elasticity. It's important to understand these in more detail. After all, the choice of line determines (above all else) your continued success with hooked fish.

Elasticity
Some stretch in nylon line is desirable; it helps to protect light hook holds from

tearing free and it avoids the sudden parting of the line when under extreme load. Regular anglers can feel the stretch in the line and know it is reaching breaking point when it locks – much like a rubber band about to break. You can stretch it just until it breaks, when it goes solid and refuses to stretch any further.

A good-quality line is expected to have a stretch percentage of 8 per cent. A 100-m length of line will therefore easily stretch when under full load and without mishap to 108m. The line regains its original length by contraction. Of this, 90 per cent returns within three hours but it may take a couple of weeks for full recovery. If a line is subjected to a loading over this inbuilt safety margin, the strain of stretch will be irreparable, although you cannot see this with the naked eye.

The amount of stretch in a given line needs to be considered when you want to sink a hook into a shark's tough jaw at long range. Too much give and the line's stretch cushions the hook, which fails to penetrate. A hard line that does not give may break on the strike. There is therefore, unfortunately, no line that is perfect for every occasion.

Tensile Strength
A line's strength is gauged by its ability to withstand longitudinal pull. This appears on the container spool as its breaking strain. Also displayed is the line's external diameter. Most breaking strains are given for a dry line. As fishing lines are used wet, it's essential to note that all mono lines weaken when submerged in water for a period of time. This loss of strength is usually between 5 and 10 per cent, but can be 15 per cent. As far as I am aware, only the ABU company give a wet-line breaking strain – the ABU test. This line breaks in water at a strain comfortably under the recognized line classes, which makes the line-class angler's

life much easier. Some specialist anglers expose other makes of line to ultra-violet light. This weakens the line's molecular structure, bringing them below a certain breaking strain – an awkward and chancy business at best.

Line diameter is really a guide as to how much line you can load onto your reel. It can also be used to indicate a breaking strain; but some brands of line now offer a higher breaking strain for a slim, overall diameter.

Line is supposed to weaken when exposed to daylight. It does, but this is marginal and, for all intents and purposes, the exposure your line gets while fishing is not a cause for concern. However, line stored at home should be kept in a dark, cool environment to avoid prolonged exposure. Extremes of heat and cold do not affect modern line to any great degree. On very cold days, line may feel a little stiffer and on hot days, slightly limp but, again this hardly alters the breaking strain.

What you should avoid is burning the line, either when retrieving it or, more likely, when a fish runs at a fast pace. Any heat should be avoided when line is passing through your fingers. Such line burn shows as a whitish, opaque scar or a few loose fibres may perhaps stand up off the line. Friction-created heat disturbs the line's molecular structure and causes a weak area. This is the most likely cause of a line break when little pressure is being exerted – a problem often wrongly blamed on the line being exposed to sunlight.

Soft lines tend to scuff and mark on the surface very easily. Stiff, hard lines are prone to fly high off the spool when you are releasing the line because of its natural springiness. This can cause backlashes and tiresome tangles.

Line Colour

Colour is less important than most anglers believe. However, I tend to stick to the clearer brands of line or go for a dark colour. I avoid fluorescent lines simply because they look so obvious. I tend to use dark lines when ledger fishing over clean sand and the clear brands when float fishing or free-lining. There seems to be no evidence of correlation between line colour and hook-ups.

Line Care

Nylon monofilament line is a wonderful material. It doesn't damage when stored correctly and, with sensible use, carries on regardless. However, it does pay to rewind line back onto a reel under even pressure after a prolonged fight with a large fish. If you wish, after a couple of trips, reverse the line – but always check the line that previously sat next to the spool for any flattening and crinkling created by crushing pressures.

If, during a session, your line has become badly twisted then, as the boat travels home, the free line should be trolled from the stern of the boat for a few minutes. When you retrieve the line, all signs of twists and kinks will have disappeared. One final point: even at sea, all discarded fishing line should either be taken home, burned, or cut into short lengths. This prevents seabirds and marine life from getting tangled in the line and stops unnecessary debris littering the seabed.

KNOTS

A very soft, limp line knots badly. When the knot is tightened, the coils cut into each other causing weakness. When a soft line is tightened to a swivel, the line that closes round the wire of the swivel's eye flattens, and this creates a second weak spot. Very stiff lines won't close when knotted. The knots can spring open and cost you fish. Both problems are usually

Figure 45: The tucked half-blood knot

Figure 46: The uni-knot

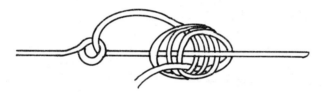

Figure 47: The Centauri knot

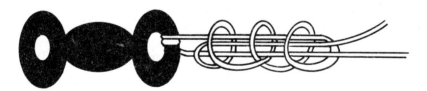

Figure 48: The double clinch knot

the result of using cheaper brands of line.

Any knot creates a weak spot. When a line is tested to the limit, it is a knot that usually breaks first. With this in mind we need to select the strongest knots but also the simpler ones that are easily tied and so reduce the risk of mistakes when tackling up under actual fishing conditions. Instead of describing the knots I use, I refer you to the figures which I'm sure are

more self-explanatory. The tucked half-blood knot is a useful and easy knot to use when attaching main reel line to upper-leader swivel. The tucked half-blood reduces the breaking strain by only 5 per cent. Exaggerated quotes of 15 per cent and more should be disregarded. If this knot gives or slips it has been tied incorrectly. In nearly thirty years of using this knot it has yet to let me down.

Another good knot is the uni-knot. This is strong and easy to tie but is a little bulky when formed. One I learnt in Australia is (I believe) called the Centauri knot. Again, this is simple to tie and very strong. It is widely used by big-game anglers. A double clinch knot serves the purpose equally well, favoured in American waters.

When anglers chase light-line records they are permitted to use up to 9m (30ft) of doubled reel line before leader attachment. This allows extra pressure to be put on a beaten fish when it nears the boat.

The advantages of a doubled line are, in my opinion, far outweighed by their disadvantages. Doubled lines are highly visible, not only when trolling but also when static fishing. The large loop has to be bound at intervals to avoid the spin and whip of the two lines in the water. Dental floss is used as whipping material for this. The dental floss and the large knot used to anchor the loop create many air bubbles as they, and the line, cut water.

The biggest headache of all is that the large knot required to form the doubled line gives poor travel through the tip ring.

On the rare occasion I've experimented with doubled line, the most efficient and easily tied knot has been the double roll knot. This is still not easy to tie when on the boat but is well worth learning. To be effective and to lock, make sure that, when the upward and downward roll of the line is complete, you twist the actual loop anti-clockwise one revolution. To tie the doubled line to the leader swivel, I use the uni-knot or the tucked half-blood, but I tighten them slowly and carefully.

Large knots that face a constant passage of water and need protection can be bound with dental floss. This gives a smooth finish, reducing water friction and disturbance. To attach the main line to the reel spool, I favour the spool knot, sometimes called the timber hitch. This is very strong and, more importantly, lies quite flat.

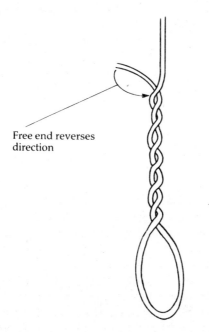

Free end reverses direction

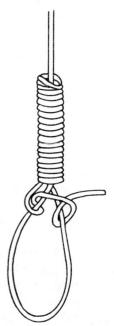

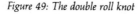

Figure 49: The double roll knot

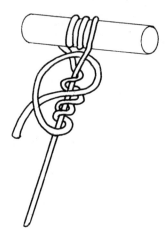

Figure 50: The spool knot

All knots should be lubricated with saliva before they are pulled tight. For extra security, you can pass the line through a swivel eye before tying any knot. This helps to spread the load. Any loose tags of line should be closely trimmed after the knot has been tightened. A well-tied knot will not slip. Loose, long tags have a habit of catching weed and other debris. When using lines of heavier grade, the tag is stiff enough to pierce the skin, which can cause a nasty wound.

LEADERS, WIRE TRACES, SWIVELS, AND LINKS

All of these need to be of the very best quality for they may have to take the full weight of the fish when the shark is brought to the side of the boat. A leader serves two main purposes: to give the crew something to hold the fish on before and during the tailing operation; and, equally importantly, to withstand any body contact caused by the shark rolling or becoming tangled with the leader. This is a frequent occurrence, so work and thought need to be applied here.

Anyone interested in records should note that the accepted length of wire trace and leader combined must not exceed 4.5m (15ft). This is a practical length for all light-line work and standard-tackle fishing. Some anglers work with a biting trace of 1m (3ft) and 4m (12ft) of lighter wire, say 115 kg (250 lb) test. I find little advantage in this, even when a shark rolls. There also seems to be a fall in bites and runs when a full wire trace is used.

I now construct my leaders from 115-kg (250-lb) commercial monofilament. This is very tough and prevents severe abrasion from contact with the shark. It is also much lighter and buoyant when a shark runs. There is also the visual aspect to consider: light mono blends better than thick wire. I distrust long lengths of wire because they can easily kink and weaken, usually parting when the shark is held close to the boat. I favour a longer-than-average biting trace, usually between 1.2 and 1.5m (4 and 5ft). This gives plenty of protection against the head and nose of the shark and, of course, it gives the teeth plenty to chew on should the shark inadvertently swallow the bait. I make my leaders as follows: a 4/0 swivel is used to connect the leader to the main line. This only takes the weight of the line load.

120

To secure any swivel, I use metal crimps (even on mono), as such a heavy grade will not knot. You slide the crimp on first then put the free end of the line through the swivel eye. This then goes over the leader to form a loop or circle. Wrap the free end through the loop twice, then go through the swivel eye and around the loop twice more. The loop is now tightened. The free end of mono goes through the crimp and is trimmed to leave a tag long enough only to double-back inside the crimp a third time. Do not allow this tag to protrude through the end of the crimp.

When actually closing the crimp, use only proper crimping pliers. Work from the centre outwards, using firm and consistent pressure. Do not, on mono, close the crimp at the very end: allow a little to be left flared at each end to avoid cutting the mono. I smooth the inside edges of crimps slightly with a tube of emery paper, whether wire or mono. This avoids any sharp edges that may cause wear. Always, when possible, use brass crimps as opposed to nickel-plated ones. The base swivel is a 6/0 Berkley or Sampo. These do actually revolve when under load – something cheaper versions do not. The Berkley is a barrel swivel available in nickel or a matt-black finish. Always go for the black version if possible. The Sampo is a ball-bearing swivel and it is quite superb in all respects. The brass torpedo swivel is a strong big-game type rarely, if ever, needed for porbeagles except when chasing record fish. I don't like any form of snap or link added to the swivel. Good ones are available, but I was once asked to test some new (and reputedly unbreakable) links made by a famous firm. These broke on a 90-kg (200-lb) fish.

I now use stainless-steel U-shackles from a chandlers. These will withstand an immense load and are fairly small. It pays to drill a fine hole in the screw end and add a little copper wire, just in case the bolt should ever try to loosen. Poor-quality swivels and snaps will undoubtedly cost you fish. The extra money spent on quality will be repaid by long, reliable service. Few traces are, in fact, actually lost while fishing.

The wire you use for the actual biting piece should be of a stainless-steel variety. Multiple-strand wire is more supple, but a shark's teeth can work in-between the individual strands, often cutting through them one at a time. I choose wire of a maximum of seven strands. This is available from several sources. Some anglers use dinghy-rigging wire but this is too much – even for sharks. Brake cable as used on racing bicycles is very good and available in lengths of up to 1.5m (5ft).

The best way to buy wire is by 100-m lengths from a commercial stockist. This

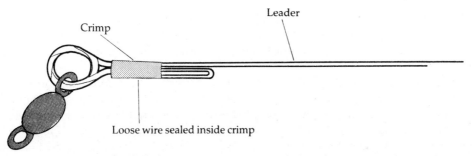

Figure 51: *Method of crimping mono or wire for leader and trace construction*

121

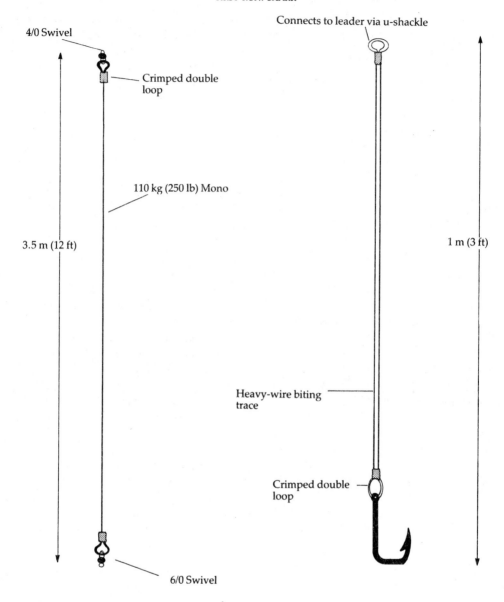

4/0 Swivel

Connects to leader via u-shackle

Crimped double
loop

110 kg (250 lb) Mono

3.5 m (12 ft)

1 m (3 ft)

Heavy-wire biting
trace

Crimped double
loop

6/0 Swivel

Figure 52: Construction of mono leader and biting trace

is much cheaper and avoids waste. Use the same system of crimping, but the top for the trace is simply a doubled loop. This accepts the shackle. The hook is attached in a similar way, again through a doubled loop. Extra care should be taken to avoid any tags of wire protruding from the crimps. Again, these can puncture the crew's hands when hauling on the trace. Also, remember to tighten the wire loops as small as possible before final crimping to improve bait presentation. My double hook rigs are just a normal single biting trace ending in a normal wire loop and hook. I then add a second length of wire from the loop that houses the first hook.

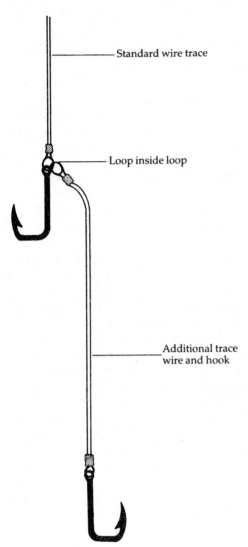

Standard wire trace

Loop inside loop

Additional trace
wire and hook

Figure 53: Standard two-hook rig

and, if you like, the wire, with pilchard oil. Avoid kinking the mono and wire during storage. I make wide, easy loops of line and wire, holding these tight with freezer-bag ties. A clear, plastic bag makes them easily identifiable and keeps them dry.

HOOKS

Relatively few hooks of varying patterns are made that are suitable for porbeagle fishing. The Mustad Seamaster is the universally accepted hook. It has caught many big fish and will, no doubt, continue to do so. In my experience, using the Seamaster, the porbeagles sometimes hold the bait in their mouths and then release it without being hooked. This happened to me several times over a couple of seasons and made me study hooks more closely.

The sharks in question were struck after the customary run and pause – anything up to ten minutes could pass before they simply let go. I had seen this happen many times with other anglers who were using the same pattern of hook. The problem is that the Seamaster has its point offset to the shank in the belief that this aids penetration. I believe the opposite to be the case.

I've been using straight-shank and point hooks exclusively now for the past six seasons and find the number of fish lost after the strike to be almost nil. I spent many fruitless hours experimenting with lines, traces, strikes, and timing. All these made no difference until I changed my hook design away from the offset point. It's possible that, when the shark shuts its mouth prior to swallowing, the hard feel created by the extra width from the offset point makes the shark cautious. Also, when a direct pull is applied to the Seamaster, it tries to twist. If the shark has eaten a length of wire, the main pull of the rod and line is being taken by the jaw,

This can be as long as you need. A second hook is then crimped to this. This simple system gives easy freedom of movement for perfect positioning.

After all trips, both the leader and the wire traces should be checked for wear and de-stranding, and then washed in warm, soapy water. Dry the leader if it is mono in a warm room, the wire trace near a stove or other heat source. Oil all swivels

which alters the angle of the wire trace as it enters the mouth. The lack of outward pull by the wire inside the mouth fails to sink the point, which eventually simply twists and falls out.

Mustad market the excellent and conventional Sea Demon. This is now my first choice for big porbeagles. When used with lines of 30 class and above, it's unbeatable. Next is the Diamond Yamamoto. This excellent Japanese hook is small for its stated size (12/0), being about the size of a normal 11/0. Nevertheless, it is a top choice for light-line work as the barb is relatively fine.

All general work can be taken on by the Mustad Bronzed O'Shaughnessy in 8/0, 10/0, and 12/0. This is the best choice when small pups are likely to be around. If necessary, these can be left in the fish in the sure knowledge that they will rot away quickly. The O'Shaughnessy has a larger-than-necessary barb. This needs reducing by filing the two edges off at right angles towards the shank's bend. This creates a sharp cutting edge that facilitates easy penetration.

Hook points are sharpened in the same way. Use a fine file, working two opposing-angled edges towards the point. When the general point is finished, hone it to peak sharpness with a fine, engineer's slip-stone and saliva. Don't over-thin the point or it may turn on contact with the jaw. To give used hooks a longer lease of life they can be cleaned of rust with fine wire-wool and then given the mandatory coating of pilchard oil. Double hooks can be useful when trolling deadbaits. I make my own from bronzed O'Shaugnessies. Cut the eye from one of the hooks and roughen the shanks with a coarse file. These are placed in a jig, side by side, with the points angled at about 40 degrees. The shanks are then brazed together. I now find it neater to cut off both eyes and weld them in a single eye from heavy-gauge

rod. The metal's temper is unimpaired if this is done correctly. They offer big advantages in instant lip-hooking. Short-shanked hooks are more difficult for a fish to throw, and they are less likely to distort through leverage when under pressure. I check the eyes of hooks used for trolling regularly for wear, as grooves can be created by the ever-moving wire.

GAFFS

Few ready-made gaffs are capable of holding a big porbeagle. It's therefore necessary to buy one designed for use on big-game fish or have one made for you. These are best used as a flying gaff. The gaff is made with a metal cup at the top with a large ring welded to it. The cup fits a metal taper on a stout alloy or wooden pole. A rope is secured to the ring, which lies flat along the length of the pole. As the gaff is sunk into the fish, the handle falls free and the rope takes the shark's weight.

The gaff itself should be constructed from at least three-eighths rod (stainless, of course), and be slightly out-turned (ie the point of the hook should be offset from the hook shank) with a deep gape. Always carry a minimum of two gaffs; three is better. As I said earlier, gaffs are barbaric – I would not use one, unless absolutely necessary.

TAILERS

You can make your own tailer from a 2-m (6-ft) length of dinghy-rigging wire or truck brake-cable. Simply create a loop at either end about 8cm (3in) long. Use heavy-duty crimps from a chandler to join the two pieces of wire. I put two crimps in tandem at both ends. Use a hammer and a very blunt chisel to seal the crimps.

Push one loop through the other, and the free loop then has 6m (20ft) of rope knotted to it. Wire sinks in water and is easier to manoeuvre over the shark's tail.

HARNESSES

Harnesses are made from either leather, canvas, or webbing. They help to spread the load away from the angler's arms by being attached to the reel lugs. Leather, being soft and supple, is the best choice. Padded linings should be of saddle felt; sponge, etc., tends to break up with prolonged use. Check all the adjustments on a harness before starting to fish, just in case you need it.

BUTT PADS

These protect the lower stomach from the pressure exerted by the rod butt. Old-fashioned stiff-leather and fibreglass designs cause pressure points on the upper thighs. Buy a modern, solid-foam version that bends to the body's shape.

Avoid buckles and fancy-fitting attachments. Ideally, harnesses should have a thin webbing belt with a plastic, seat-belt type clip. A plain cup of plastic or fibreglass for the rod's butt cap to fit into is all that is necessary for shark-fishing.

GENERAL STORAGE

All the items of tackle you need to carry should be stowed in a plastic, water-tight box. Many companies make suitable models, particularly Daiwa and the American company, Plano. These are probably the best I've ever come across. Reels can be placed in the base, with hooks, leaders, and traces, etc., placed in the trays. There's usually ample room for all your waterproofs as well. Cantilever boxes are useful in that they give you instant location of needed items. Select a model with a locking lid as these have been known to fly open, spilling all their contents when lifted. Use a strong, webbing strap with a solid loop that goes around the whole box when you need to lower gear from a jetty to the boat. Tackle is frequently lost or broken in this way by anglers who trust to luck.

I like to carry a knife when out at sea, and this does not need to be huge and cumbersome. A small knife housed in a belt-pouch is adequate, and a useful tool to have to hand when things go wrong and ropes get tangled. A basic first-aid kit is essential when shark-fishing. Aim to carry plasters and bandage, antiseptic cream, small scissors and tweezers. Sharks seem to have an anti-coagulant on their teeth — any wounds bleed in a persistent manner, so cleaning them is a priority.

CHAPTER 15

Some General Advice

Many things have an indirect bearing on the numbers of fish we catch. For example, in chapter 2 we saw how the porbeagle is able to pick up small electrical signals given out by baitfish. In the same way, it has been noted that all kinds of sharks have a tendency to approach the side of the boat that carries the batteries or other electrical equipment more frequently. This observation comes from discussions with both charter captains and commercial fishers. This can be taken further. Most shark boats I've known to have been bumped by porbeagles have had steel hulls. Small electric fields that exist through decay of the metal may help draw the shark.

Many experiments have been carried out that have proved that sharks respond to particular sounds. A few companies now make a device that can be lowered into the water while you fish. This gives off controlled sound waves that can be adjusted to different levels. Whether these actually work or not I do not know, but the idea is logical and worth pursuing.

TROPHIES

Any large shark you catch and bring home for weighing will obviously be a special fish for you. Photographs are the usual way of holding the memory, but I've never been happy with the great-white-

hunter poses, as these tend to lose something over the years. You can, however, try to preserve the jaws, teeth, and so on. The method so often seen, where the jaws are boiled in water to remove all the meat, fails to work on porbeagles. Porbeagles' jaws are made of pure cartilage and will soften when boiled: the teeth literally drop out. Burying them in the garden and relying on worms to remove the flesh is also unsuccessful. The dampness in the soil softens the cartilage, which then rots. Simply removing the flesh and allowing the jaws to air-dry is also a poor technique. The jaws eventually begin to decay and to smell.

The most successful method is as follows. The head section needs to be on a solid structure with a non-slip surface. Place the head upside down and begin cutting the skin and flesh away from the lower jaw. Work in slow, short strokes avoiding any contact with the jaw or teeth. When all the flesh has been removed from the lower jaw, cut a deep slit towards the hinge of the top and bottom jaw. Now work the knife along the outer edge of the top jaw from hinge to hinge. Next, score a line with the knife from between the eyes towards the point of the nose, and to either side of the eyes. Begin to ease the flesh away, little by little, using shallow cuts until the jaw is reached. Keep paring away until all the flesh is removed and release the jaws. All remaining flesh can be taken off by a knife and a stiff toothbrush.

Next we need to dry and seal the jaws. A solution of 1 part formalin to 40 parts water does the job. However, care is needed as recent reports of possible side-effects are worrying. Rubber gloves and a breathing-mask will alleviate most fears. The clean, dry jaws should be immersed fully in this solution of formalin and water for five days. They can then be removed and left to dry. When fully dry, you can coat them with a clear varnish. This retards the decay process but is not permanent. If you have the facilities for permanent immersion, the jaws should be taken out of the formalin and placed in industrial methylated spirits or neat alcohol of the preserving kind. The professional preservation of soft jaws is beyond the scope of this book.

SEABIRDS

Seabirds' antics can aid the angler: when the fishing is quiet and the usual marks fail to produce, note the seabirds that fly in a purposeful manner. A trip in the same direction may locate a shoal of baitfish with their attendant porbeagles. Gannets and other species will often circle a particular area. They won't dive for food yet refuse to leave. I've often wondered if this is because of the presence of sharks. When fishing an area where gannets are airborne but not feeding, as soon as we've stopped and lowered baits into the water the result has been an instant run.

Seabirds also smell the odour of the chum trail and come to sit in the middle of it, taking small pieces of floating fish. If you take careful note, the seagulls will lift from the water just before you get a shark run. They are obviously aware of the shark's presence and leave for the safety of the air. Also, when sharks are not feeding but circling the boat, no seagulls are on the water. Intriguingly, when a shark is hooked and fighting, seabirds will re-settle on the water quite happily.

This also applies to a shark left on the boat overnight. You would expect the local seabirds to have a field-day, but this is not the case. The birds refuse even to sit on the vessel that houses the shark. However, when the shark is gutted and steaked, they instantly devour any offal. I've never come across probeagles eating seagulls, but these experiences suggest a definite wariness on the birds' part.

RECORDS

I've always kept a diary of catches and, more importantly, blank days. Much of what my diary says has helped me write this book. Days when no sharks are caught can teach you as much as the more successful ones. I make sure to note down the following: location; ground composition; wind direction and strength; cloud cover or hours of sunshine; water clarity; sea state; air temperature and sea temperature; size and strength of tide; the weather patterns from the last couple of days; and other boats' results.

With regards to the shark, I note the depth at which any runs occurred, looking for a favoured depth, and the exact time at which the runs came. I've already mentioned that dusk and dawn are good, but morning fish are rare. This could be because of the need to establish the chum trail and to give it time to work. Midday, when light from the sun is more direct, is a favourable time, but smaller fish are more likely. Full afternoon produces good fish, but bigger fish have a habit of showing after 4 p.m. – they are more inclined to feed at this time. Big fish will often swim in full view of the boat during the day but not feed. As the light levels begin to fall, they suddenly switch on and take a bait.

Diaries take time to prove their worth. After a few seasons, patterns emerge that help the angler to formulate new ideas and develop more efficient techniques.

When a fish is to be weighed, keep it wet at all times: sharks can lose valuable weight when exposed to hot, drying winds. They can also lose weight when you lift them by the tail. Blood and body juices can pour from the mouth. Where possible, suspend the dead shark which is to be weighed by placing a gaff hook through the lower jaw.

For identification purposes, photographs should be taken in both black and white and colour. Get a full-length shot of the shark and close-ups of the dorsal, pectoral, and tail fins, and the head and mouth. Make sure you have a person in one photo by whom you can gauge the total length. Measure accurately the full length from the tip of the nose to the inner cleft of the tail. Measure the girth from just in front of the dorsal and to the rear of the pectorals. For my own records I also measure the height of the dorsal.

Porbeagles don't grow to a standard form. Some are long, thin fish, while others are short and fat. A table of sizes and weights therefore serves no purpose. As they get heavier, porbeagles increase their girth to a greater degree than their length. In the case of record fish, ensure you have the names and addresses of at least two independent witnesses. It is most important to retain the jaws, as the teeth are the mandatory form of identification, and to get the scales checked and issued with a certificate of validation. Keep a copy of all things, and register all mail.

CHAPTER 16

Conservation: Responsible Angling

Apart from very much larger sharks, the porbeagle has nothing to fear in its natural environment. Only we have the ability, aggression, and intelligence to capture such a supreme fish. We also, of course, pollute the waters in which it swims, destroy its food supply, and kill it for use as fertilizers and food. Porbeagles are good to eat. However, simply being a shark has helped to keep its consumption down because of the misbelief that sharks are scavengers that eat anything.

In parts of southern Europe, porbeagle has been marketed as mock swordfish. The Portuguese are fond of porbeagle meat. There is a large fishery in Portuguese waters, but vessels travel far afield in the search for *Lamna* – as far as the Irish Sea and off the west coast of Ireland. The fishing method employed uses mile after mile of long lines. The shark takes the bait and is gut-hooked and, being unable to swim, it quickly drowns.

The Norwegians probably controlled the biggest long-lining operation from the mid-1950s to the early 1970s. At the peak of production, over nine million tons of porbeagle were processed. Much of this fishing took place in the waters off the north-west of Ireland. Knowing that porbeagles are to some extent territorial, it is no surprise to learn that catch returns quickly diminished. Only 2–4 young are born to each female porbeagle at any one time. Porbeagles have a very slow rate of growth – only 20cm (8in) in length per year. These factors soon made the industry uneconomical as boats were pushed further and further afield and running costs soared.

The meat from this fishery was almost totally exported to Italy, where shark meat (known as *smerglio*) is highly prized. Recently it has become fashionable to eat shark. The greater demand has created an increase in price, which has offset the difficulty of locating the fish, and consequently more sharks are killed.

A worrying trend in all forms of commercial fishing is the high number of small pups taken. Small fish are naturally the majority: they lack the power and tenacity to break free. A nursery-area can be quickly decimated.

The quickest way to destroy a species is to wipe out its food source. This is well underway with the porbeagle's principal food sources of mackerel and herring. In the British Isles, the once-prolific mackerel shoals have been dramatically reduced. The days when the whole surface of the sea would boil have long since past. Some summers they hardly show at all and, if they do, they are small, joey mackerel, not the big, fat fish of old. British catch returns are less than half what they were 20 years ago. If the fish are located, modern techniques can take in a day that which would have kept an old-fashioned trawler working for a full month.

This applies equally to the coast of Maine and North Bay, where the American fishery used to salt in excess of 500,000 barrels each season. The shoals in this area could be 20 miles (30km) long and over half a mile wide. Such shoals are long gone. Mackerel are slow to mature. They reach maturity at a length of 30cm (12in) and 3–4 years of age. A female will lay half-a-million eggs each year, but only two or three of these will survive to reach maturity. It's easy to see why the shoals are decreasing.

It's much the same story for the herring. The Atlantic herring-catch tonnage has fallen from over four million tons to under one million tons. The sharpest fall has been in the heart of porbeagle territory where Norwegian and Icelandic catches have fallen from two million tons to only 200,000 tons.

Whitefish catches are also in decline. Remedial action in the form of species bans and limiting catch tonnage over a given period of time only scratches the surface of the problem. The figures quoted are for landings. Fish are still caught and simply thrown back over the side where they die because of the rapid change in pressure. Porbeagles are adaptable but, in order to live, their whole life pattern, habits, breeding cycle, and growth rate may have to change. This is a situation we must do our utmost to avoid.

Pollutants also have a hand to play. There are five major groups of toxins that cause concern: radio-active particles, petroleum products, halogenated hydrocarbons, heavy metals, and litter, such as plastics. Also of concern is the amount of untreated domestic sewage being pumped into the sea. This contains very high levels of nutrients that encourage the rapid growth of plankton over wide areas. This rapid growth of plankton uses the available oxygen in the water for, as it dies and falls to the seabed, the bacteria that

normally digest it cannot cope with the quantities. The residue rots and, in decay, consumes the oxygen. Fish move out of the area, along with the rest of the food chain. Plankton blooms might also become more common as the seas warm because of the greenhouse effect.

In the face of such awesome potential for destruction of the marine environment, what can we, as anglers, do to help? The answer, of course, is to do the little we can to preserve the species, as we participate in our chosen sport. Never take a fish that will not be eaten, and when you do, have a target weight of at least 45 kg (100 lb). Ensure everything possible is done at the side of the boat to keep a shark as calm as possible until the trace and hook are cut free. Use only bronzed hooks when fish are to be returned. These rot quickly and soon fall out. If for any reason a fish has to be lifted into the boat, do try to support the tail, stomach, and head. This helps to protect the shark's internal organs, which rely on the surrounding water for support. When placing such a fish back in the water, do so gently. Never drop the fish over the gunnel. Support the shark by the tail as it goes back and let it get re-adjusted to the water before letting it go. It will swim away after a few seconds.

Don't listen to stories that porbeagles can't recover and hence die after being played on rod and line. I've seen fish return to the same area after being captured and released to take another bait. Body scars are distinctive enough to identify individual sharks. Many shark boats are full of photographs depicting fish being unceremoniously dragged over the gunnels, by either the wire trace or at the wrong end of a gaff. Some angling magazines and journalists delight in this brutal type of photography. Such shots devalue the sport. Photograph your fish in the water where they belong, prior to release, or on the boat or back at the quay in the case of a special fish when it is well and truly dead. I also make a point of washing off any blood that seeps naturally from a dead shark before I take any colour photographs. Such effects create the wrong impression to the casual bystander and, again, distort the image of angling.

Never gut a shark in full view of tourists or casual onlookers. At best it's a gory business and should be kept for the eyes of those who need to be there. Dispose of any waste sensibly – don't leave it in full view. Either seal it in a non-transparent plastic bag or, better still, dump the remains at sea.

Never allow too much information on the location of any captures to leak out, either from yourself, or your companions. Commercial fishers are quick to capitalize on such useful information, as will other shark skippers and their parties. As we have seen, the porbeagle will return to the same grounds and at the same time of year, usually within a few days of the same date. Commercial skippers have good memories and keep diaries. Many top-class charter captains never let information be broadcast over the radio, for such a blunder sees both pleasure and commercial craft converge on the area. Some skippers even set the navigation co-ordinates slightly off so that anyone on board with less than genuine intentions cannot profit from selfish vigilance.

Glossary

AMPULLAE   Sac-like structures receptive to electrical fields. They are situated around the shark's snout just beneath the skin. Sharks may well attack boats because of the electrical fields they produce.

CENTRUM   The body of a vertebra.

CHUM   American name for rubby dubby.

CLASPERS   Male shark's reproductive organs; (yes, there are two).

CLOACA   Excretory opening; in the female it combines genital and excretory functions.

CUSP   Small projecting fangs at base of the main tooth designed for gripping.

CYALUME   Type of light stick used to attract predatory fish.

DEMERSAL   Being on, or living near, the sea bed.

DENTICLES   Thorn-like structures on a shark's skin. (Sharks do not have scales, as do bony fish).

DROGUE   Device towed by the boat to reduce the speed of a tidal drift.

EPILIMNION   Area of warm water above thermocline.

GILL ARCH   A structure of the throat that supports gill tissue.

HETERO-CERCAL   A fish tail with the spinal column curving upwards to form the upper lobe of a two-lobed structure.

HYPO-LIMNION   Area of cold water below thermocline.

JAPANESE BIRDS   Surface skipping lure trolled from a powered boat.

KONA   Type of artificial lure trolled from a powered boat.

LAMNIDAE   Scientific family name for the group of sharks which includes porbeagles. This group contains two other genera: *Carcharodon*, the great white, and *Isurus*, the mackerel shark. (Shark classification is forever being reviewed; the porbeagle family has been called *Isuridae*.)

LATERAL LINE   Sensory system running the full flank of the shark, sensitive to movement in the water. Detection of vibration through the lateral line is sometimes called 'distant touch'.

LEADER   Length of wire or heavy mono between hook trace and main line designed to withstand contact with a shark's tail or skin.

LEDGERING To fish a bait hard on the seabed using a lead weight.

NEURAL ARCH Arch-shaped structure at the top of a vertebra that shields the spinal cord.

NOTO-CHORD Component of spinal column.

OPERCULAR Single gill cover of a normal fish as opposed to the several gill slits found on a shark.

OSTEO-BLASTS Cells around which depositing of calcium salts creates bone.

OSTEOCYTES Cells found in bone as a derivative of osteoblasts.

OVIDUCT Canal through which eggs pass in female shark.

OVOVIVI-PAROUS Producing young by means of egg hatching and developing inside the mother. Young rely on a yolk sac and cannibalism of other, less developed young inside the womb for nourishment. Porbeagles are ovoviviparous.

PELAGIC Belonging to the upper surface of the sea.

PIRKS Hollow metal tubes filled with lead. Worked in an up-and-down motion of the rod tip; its vibrations attract fish.

PLUGS Plastic or wooden artificial lures incorporating a plastic lip to imitate more closely a swimming action. Larger varieties attract shark.

RAPALA PLUGS A specific brand of plug with a noted reputation for attracting small shark.

ROSTRUM Supporting cartilage situated in the nose of the shark.

RUBBY DUBBY Mixture of oily fish finely minced and added to bran and pilchard oil. This is placed in fine weave bags and hung over the side of the boat. The resultant slick or smell in the water ultimately draws the shark in to feed.

SNOOD Length of line between a junction of tackle and a hook.

SOUND Angler's term to describe the action of a shark who dives deep.

SPOON Metal lure shaped like a spoon, usually trolled behind boat.

TAPETUM Reflective layer positioned behind the retina of the eye. This reflects light back through the retina; a useful adaptation in dim light. In bright light, however such a mechanism would dazzle the shark. To prevent this, each of the silvery platelets that form the tapetum is covered with cells containing dark pigment. This spreads out as the shark encounters bright light (on the surface); an effective pair of sunglasses.

THERMO-CLINE Dividing line between two temperatures of water.

TROLL To tow a bait at a specific speed behind a powered boat to induce a fish to feed.

VIVIPAROUS Young are retained within the mother until full development and nourished by a placental connection to the uterine wall.

Index

Page references in *italics* refer to diagrams.